Nuclear Power

Other Books of Related Interest

Opposing Viewpoints Series

Coal
Doomsday Scenarios
Energy Alternatives
NASA

At Issue Series

The BP Oil Spill
Nuclear and Toxic Waste
Weapons of War

Current Controversies Series

Nuclear Armament
Nuclear Energy

"Congress shall make no law … abridging the freedom of speech, or of the press."

First Amendment to the US Constitution

The basic foundation of our democracy is the First Amendment guarantee of freedom of expression. The Opposing Viewpoints Series is dedicated to the concept of this basic freedom and the idea that it is more important to practice it than to enshrine it.

Nuclear Power

Lynn M. Zott and Helga Schier, Book Editors

GREENHAVEN PRESS
A part of Gale, Cengage Learning

Detroit • New York • San Francisco • New Haven, Conn • Waterville, Maine • London

Elizabeth Des Chenes, *Director, Publishing Solutions*

For more information, contact:
Greenhaven Press
27500 Drake Rd.
Farmington Hills, MI 48331-3535
Or you can visit our Internet site at gale.cengage.com.

Articles in Greenhaven Press anthologies are often edited for length to meet page requirements. In addition, original titles of these works are changed to clearly present the main thesis and to explicitly indicate the author's opinion. Every effort is made to ensure that Greenhaven Press accurately reflects the original intent of the authors. Every effort has been made to trace the owners of copyrighted material.

LIBRARY OF CONGRESS CATALOGING-IN-PUBLICATION DATA

Nuclear power / Lynn M. Zott and Helga Schier, book editors.
p. cm. -- (Opposing viewpoints)
Includes bibliographical references and index.
ISBN 978-0-7377-6062-0 (hardcover) -- ISBN 978-0-7377-6063-7 (pbk.)
1. Nuclear energy. 2. Nuclear energy--Safety measures. 3. Nuclear energy--Economic aspects. 4. Nuclear power plants--Risk assessment. 5. Nuclear power plants--Safety measures. I. Zott, Lynn M. (Lynn Marie), 1969– II. Schier, Helga.
TK9008.N83 2012
333.792'4--dc23

2012024695

Printed in the United States of America
1 2 3 4 5 6 7 16 15 14 13 12

Contents

Chapter 2: Is Nuclear Power Good for the Environment?

Chapter 3: Is Nuclear Power an Economical Source of Energy?

Why Consider Opposing Viewpoints?

> *"The only way in which a human being can make some approach to knowing the whole of a subject is by hearing what can be said about it by persons of every variety of opinion and studying all modes in which it can be looked at by every character of mind. No wise man ever acquired his wisdom in any mode but this."*
>
> *John Stuart Mill*

In our media-intensive culture it is not difficult to find differing opinions. Thousands of newspapers and magazines and dozens of radio and television talk shows resound with differing points of view. The difficulty lies in deciding which opinion to agree with and which "experts" seem the most credible. The more inundated we become with differing opinions and claims, the more essential it is to hone critical reading and thinking skills to evaluate these ideas. Opposing Viewpoints books address this problem directly by presenting stimulating debates that can be used to enhance and teach these skills. The varied opinions contained in each book examine many different aspects of a single issue. While examining these conveniently edited opposing views, readers can develop critical thinking skills such as the ability to compare and contrast authors' credibility, facts, argumentation styles, use of persuasive techniques, and other stylistic tools. In short, the Opposing Viewpoints Series is an ideal way to attain the higher-level thinking and reading skills so essential in a culture of diverse and contradictory opinions.

In addition to providing a tool for critical thinking, Opposing Viewpoints books challenge readers to question their own strongly held opinions and assumptions. Most people form their opinions on the basis of upbringing, peer pressure, and personal, cultural, or professional bias. By reading carefully balanced opposing views, readers must directly confront new ideas as well as the opinions of those with whom they disagree. This is not to argue simplistically that everyone who reads opposing views will—or should—change his or her opinion. Instead, the series enhances readers' understanding of their own views by encouraging confrontation with opposing ideas. Careful examination of others' views can lead to the readers' understanding of the logical inconsistencies in their own opinions, perspective on why they hold an opinion, and the consideration of the possibility that their opinion requires further evaluation.

Evaluating Other Opinions

To ensure that this type of examination occurs, Opposing Viewpoints books present all types of opinions. Prominent spokespeople on different sides of each issue as well as well-known professionals from many disciplines challenge the reader. An additional goal of the series is to provide a forum for other, less known, or even unpopular viewpoints. The opinion of an ordinary person who has had to make the decision to cut off life support from a terminally ill relative, for example, may be just as valuable and provide just as much insight as a medical ethicist's professional opinion. The editors have two additional purposes in including these less known views. One, the editors encourage readers to respect others' opinions—even when not enhanced by professional credibility. It is only by reading or listening to and objectively evaluating others' ideas that one can determine whether they are worthy of consideration. Two, the inclusion of such viewpoints encourages the important critical thinking skill of objectively evaluating an author's credentials and bias. This evaluation will illuminate an author's reasons for taking a particular stance on an issue and will aid in readers' evaluation of the author's ideas.

It is our hope that these books will give readers a deeper understanding of the issues debated and an appreciation of the complexity of even seemingly simple issues when good and honest people disagree. This awareness is particularly important in a democratic society such as ours in which people enter into public debate to determine the common good. Those with whom one disagrees should not be regarded as enemies but rather as people whose views deserve careful examination and may shed light on one's own.

Thomas Jefferson once said that "difference of opinion leads to inquiry, and inquiry to truth." Jefferson, a broadly educated man, argued that "if a nation expects to be ignorant and free . . . it expects what never was and never will be." As individuals and as a nation, it is imperative that we consider the opinions of others and examine them with skill and discernment. The Opposing Viewpoints Series is intended to help readers achieve this goal.

David L. Bender and Bruno Leone,
Founders

Introduction

> *"I'd like to have a society work without nuclear as early as possible. . . . But as to in reality how quickly it can be reduced or whether it will ultimately be reduced to zero—I want to judge based on discussion by experts."*
>
> *Yukio Edano, energy minister, Japan*

On March 11, 2011, disaster struck in Japan. A 9.0 magnitude earthquake shook the country, unleashing a massive tsunami that flooded the coast and leveled everything in its path. Aftershocks rumbled through the islands, fires sprang up, and an explosion at the Fukushima Daiichi Nuclear Power Plant sent shock waves of fear around the world that still reverberate. The earthquake and tsunami caused a series of power outages and equipment failures, which in turn caused a series of nuclear meltdowns in three of six reactors at Daiichi. Radiation was released, and the area had to be evacuated. The Fukushima disaster was categorized as a Level 7 on the International Nuclear Events Scale, the highest level possible.

The Fukushima disaster reignited an age-old controversy over nuclear power: Should nuclear fission reactors be used to generate electricity for civilian purposes? On the international stage, opinions oscillate between two extremes.

Two weeks after the disaster in Japan, on March 26, 2011, more than 250,000 Germans marched the streets carrying slogans such as "Heed Fukushima—shut off all nuclear plants." Citing safety concerns with aging nuclear plants, Germany took its eight oldest reactors offline only weeks after Fukushima, and two months later, on May 30, 2011, Chancellor Angela Merkel announced that the country would phase out nuclear power and shut down the remaining nine reactors by 2022. This set in motion a huge shift in the country's energy policy. Germany will have to invest heavily in renewable energies to guarantee the necessary power supply *without* reverting to the use of fossil fuels.

Citing national energy independence and security, as well as an obligation to reducing greenhouse gas emissions, France has no plans to phase out nuclear power, which provides more than 75 percent of the country's electricity. Instead, the government under President Nicolas Sarkozy has renewed its commitment to this energy sector and ordered the inspection of all its nuclear power facilities to evaluate the potential risks involved in case of natural disasters, accidents, or human failures and to develop improvements in safety and security procedures.

And what about Japan? According to the *New York Times*'s Martin Fackler: "All but two of . . . 54 commercial reactors have gone offline since the nuclear disaster a year ago [2011], after the earthquake and tsunami, and it is not clear when they can be restarted. With the last operating reactor scheduled to be idled as soon as next month [April 2012], Japan—once one of the world's leaders in atomic energy—will have at least temporarily shut down an industry that once generated a third of its electricity." Nevertheless, the Japanese government has renewed its commitment to nuclear power, albeit with a caveat: "We cannot say yes to restarts until we are certain that they are absolutely safe," explains Shiga Prefecture Governor Yukiko Kada, and Energy Minister Yukio Edano would prefer to end the country's reliance on nuclear power, but admits that this might be unrealistic in the near future.

Amidst the safety concerns highlighted by the Fukushima disaster, the nuclear debate in the United States has become more contentious. Proponents of nuclear power such as Charles Ferguson in *Nature* argue that "phasing out nuclear power worldwide would be an overreaction. It provides about 15 percent of global electricity and even larger percentages in certain countries, such as France (almost 80 percent) and the United States (about 20 percent). Eliminating nuclear power would lead to much greater use of fossil fuels, and raise greenhouse-gas emissions. It will probably take at least a few decades to massively scale up use of renewable sources. Meanwhile, nuclear plants can bridge the energy gap." Mitch Singer from the Nuclear Energy Institute argues a similar point: "There are plenty of studies showing that nuclear is key in providing baseload power. . . . Wind and solar are so variable they really present a problem when you put that much on the grid."

Consequently, the Barack Obama administration's 2012 budget proposes to advance both renewable energy sources as well as the next generation of nuclear power plants. As Rocky Barker reports in *Voices*: "[The] Department of Energy . . . will set up cost-sharing agreements with private industry to design and license small modular nuclear reactors. . . . These reactors would be one-third the size of current nuclear plants and be designed with inherent safety, siting, construction and economic benefits." While nuclear power might pose safety risks, its proponents argue it needs to be part of the energy mix of the future, because in contrast to the chief alternative of fossil fuel, it produces virtually no air pollution and is therefore the only viable energy source that can provide reliable national energy independence while not contributing to global warming.

Opponents of nuclear power contradict the claim that nuclear power is environmentally friendly by pointing to the entire nuclear fuel chain, which includes uranium mining, the long process of decommissioning nuclear plants and the unresolved issue of nuclear waste storage. Small modular reactors such as those supported by the Obama administration would still grapple with these issues. Therefore opponents of nuclear power favor a complete phase-out, citing the need to transform the national energy system to sustainable energy sources. Timeforchange.org, an environmental protection group, argues that if the United States relies on nuclear energy, such a transformation will never take place. "We cannot on one hand decide to continue nuclear power to generate electricity and on the other hand expect alternatives to be developed."

The authors in *Opposing Viewpoints: Nuclear Power* take a close look at the safety, environmental, and financial concerns that characterize the nuclear debate in the following chapters: Can the Risks Involved in Nuclear Power Be Managed?, Is Nuclear Power Good for the Environment?, and Is Nuclear Power an Economical Source of Energy?

Chapter 1

Can the Risks Involved in Nuclear Power Be Managed?

Chapter Preface

The Indian Point Nuclear Power plant is located about thirty miles north of New York City in Buchanan, New York. The plant's two reactors went online in 1962, with an original license to operate until 2014. In 2007 Entergy Corporation, which owns and operates the plant, applied for a twenty-year extension on its license. The extension faces strong opposition, particularly since the March 2011 disaster at the Fukushima nuclear power plant in Japan.

New York State Assemblyman Richard Brodsky summarizes the concerns: "Indian Point is dangerous. Earthquake faults underneath, terrorism vulnerability, fire safety defects, unworkable evacuation plans, aging equipment, spent fuel deposits . . . have combined to present an unacceptable level of danger. The chances of a significant meltdown at Indian Point remain small; the consequences are so terrifyingly immense that it can't be tolerated." Brodsky holds that the plant should "never have been built so close to NYC and 20 million people and could not be built there under today's rules." According to Brodsky, the plant's location near a metropolitan area alone is reason enough not to renew its operating license. As Fukushima has shown, a nuclear meltdown might require the evacuation of a ten to fifty mile radius, which at Indian Point translates into the evacuation of up to 20 million people, an impossible endeavor with immeasurable economic and social repercussions.

Entergy, the plant's operator, argues that the "Indian Point Energy Center generates 2,000 megawatts of electricity, or 20 percent to 40 percent of the electric power used in our area depending on time of year and load on the grid. The facility provides power to millions of homes," employs more than 1,100 people, and is therefore vital to the economy of the New York metropolitan area. If the plants were to be shut down, not only would energy prices rise by up to 12 percent, but "up to 2.1 million customers in southern New York would be vulnerable to power interruptions from 2016 to 2020," says Rick Gonzales, chief operating officer of the New York Independent System Operator, which runs the state's power grid.

Riverkeeper, an environmental group focused on protecting "the environmental, recreational and commercial integrity of the Hudson River and its tributaries," fights for a permanent shut down of the plant due to clean water act violations following a 2010 accident at the plant. Riverkeeper argues that the plant does not comply with safety regulations, possibly due to cost cutting measures and the plant's advanced age. The plant's operators counter that "nuclear plants always have components that break and need to be replaced," and "while the external buildings may be 40 years old, the plants at Indian Point are continually being upgraded and strengthened and we have invested over a billion dollars to do so in recent years."

Countering the argument that Indian Point should be shut down due to its location on fault lines, the plant's operators claim that the plant is "rated to withstand an earthquake of at least a 6.0 magnitude on the Richter scale. In fact, due to design and construction conservatisms, we are confident that Indian Point can withstand greater than a 7.0 magnitude earthquake," a magnitude much higher than has ever been recorded at that location. The plant operators argue that they are prepared for the risks inherent in the plant's location: "We don't say 'it can't happen here' and simply ignore possible scenarios. In fact, we plan and train every day to expect the unexpected."

Despite such safety assurances from the plant operators, New York Governor Andrew Cuomo calls for Indian Point to be shut down permanently, in part due to its potential vulnerability to terrorism, an issue of particular importance to the area since the 9/11 terrorist attacks.

Amidst news from the aftermath of the Fukushima disaster, calls for the closure of Indian Point have intensified. The unimaginable might happen at any given power plant at any time.

The question is how the risk of the unimaginable is evaluated and whether it is a risk that should be taken given the benefits of nuclear power plants. The viewpoints in this chapter explore whether the risks inherent in using nuclear power can be managed, the frequency of adverse events involving nuclear reactors, whether exposure to radiation has negative effects, whether advances in design and safety precautions can address major threats and security concerns, and whether spent nuclear fuel can be safely and securely stored.

Viewpoint 1

"Fukushima was . . . a dramatic example that the risks imposed by accepting the benefits of affordable, emission free nuclear energy are well within the 'acceptable' range."

The Fukushima Disaster Proves That Nuclear Power Risks Are Manageable

Rod Adams

In the following viewpoint Rod Adams argues that anti-nuclear activists have exaggerated the scale of disaster at the Fukushima power plants. A closer look at the events, Adams explains, reveals that the newer reactors at the site, which had improved power supply systems, withstood the earthquake and tsunami and could be shut down safely. This suggests, according to Adams, that it is possible to build nuclear power plants that are safer and more sustainable than competing sources of energy. Adams is a pro-nuclear power activist with experience in operating nuclear plants.

As you read, consider the following questions:

1. Which two natural events caused the nuclear power crisis in Fukushima, Japan, according to the viewpoint?

Rod Adams, "Fukushima Happened. Now What?," *Atomic Insights*, December 19, 2011.

2. What does Adams argue was possible due to an improved power supply system?
3. How did providers of non-nuclear energy sources react to the disaster in Fukushima, according to Adams?

In the months and years to come, post-Fukushima,[1] people who influence power plant construction decisions will be making choices that will have a large impact on future generations. In this reflective time of the year, it is important to gather the most accurate lessons learned and to offer some food for thought about the motives that might be leading some decision makers to completely misread the lessons that should be learned.

What Really Happened at Fukushima

In March 2011, an enormous earthquake shook the north east coast of Japan. It rattled every part of the infrastructure, including several large nuclear power stations. Many parts of the infrastructure were seriously damaged by the earth's movement. Apparently, all of the nuclear power stations were able to safely shut down and suffered no long term damage from the shaking.

The earth's movement also generated a large tidal wave (tsunami) that reached heights as high as 45 feet (14 meters) in some places. That wave washed over the defenses that had been engineered to protect the people, factories, buildings, bridges, and ports that tend to concentrate in various parts of the coast all around the world.

There are many benefits for human society that are associated with living close to the ocean; there is a good reason why about 75% of the world's population lives within 50 miles of the coast. There is also, however, a certain amount of risk associated with living near the ocean. Sometimes, it causes enormous damage as it surges over the structures that humans have erected.

That wave (actually multiple waves) of salt water severely damaged nearly everything in its path. The tsunami's wide path included the sites of two large nuclear power stations in the

Fukushima prefecture, one with six individual units (Daiichi—aka First) and one with four slightly newer units just a few miles away (Daini—aka Second).

Disaster Prevention at the Daini Nuclear Plants

At Daiichi, there were two groupings of nuclear units—a group of four right on the coast, and a group of two that were on slightly higher ground. Those two separate units were part of the last phase of the station construction; they included some refinements compared to the units that had been built in the earliest phases.

Daini (the second station in Fukushima) also included design refinements that had been suggested during construction at Daiichi, the plants were on slightly higher ground and the emergency power system was not quite so concentrated in basements and low lying portions of the plant site. As nukes [experts in nuclear power] would describe it, there was more "separation" and more "diversity" in the backups to the backup power supply.

We all "know" what happened to four of the units at Daiichi, the first nuclear station built in the Fukushima prefecture. The tsunami wiped out the plant's primary power supply (the electrical grid) and wiped out nearly all of the backup power supplies (at least 8 of them). The wave also washed into the basements of the power plant buildings including the ones at each unit that housed the switchgear where the emergency diesel generators connected to the plant's electrical power systems.

As a direct result of an insufficiently diverse and separated electrical power supply system, four units at Daiichi lost the ability to circulate water, the ability to add water, the ability to ventilate the secondary containment structures to prevent pockets of hydrogen from accumulating, and the ability to monitor the conditions of the plants. The loss of those important capabilities, all enabled by having some form of electrical power available, led to the often repeated stories of significant plant damage and the release of easily sensed quantities of radioactive material.

The improved power supply systems at the newest two units at Fukushima Daiichi and the four units at Fukushima Daini allowed the operators at those facilities to put them into a safe, cooled down condition without releasing any radioactive material to the environment.

Reactions to the Events in Japan

In the aftermath of the earthquake and tsunami, the developed world's public consciousness was quickly directed to focus on the slowly developing events that were happening at one of the nuclear power stations that had been affected by the twin natural disasters. There is nothing automatic about that focusing; it was the result of thousands of individual editorial and production decisions about which facet of the story to cover.

The individuals who made those decisions had to consciously or unconsciously weigh the importance and the value of telling everyone more about the nuclear power plant woes (often filling valuable air time and print space by repeating the same story and the same video footage hundreds to thousands of times) while *not* telling them about the public suffering due to loss of family members, housing, income generating property, or about the woes at other industrial facilities—like the Cosmo oil refinery in Chiba [Japan] that experienced a dramatic and photogenic fire [on March 11, 2011] that raged uncontrolled for 10 solid days.

Antinuclear activists around the world leaped into action to emphasize the events and even to spin tall tales about the possible "worst case" accidents. They are still working that story as hard as they can. . . .

Antinuclear Activists Exaggerate the Scale of the Disaster

One particular Manchurian candidate [a political candidate supporting a particular group to win an election] activist who had fairly recently been appointed to a key strategic position as the head of the US Nuclear Regulatory Commission, the widely recognized "gold standard" of government nuclear safety experts, testified to the US Congress that the situation at the power station was so bad that all Americans within 50 miles of the plant needed to evacuate.

That pronouncement has been repeated thousands of times and is often being used as the justification for actions to shut down existing nuclear plants that are within 50 miles of a large, difficult to evacuate population concentration.

Other lifelong antinuclear activists in public office took to the air waves and made dramatic statements about the tragedy and about the need to quickly move away from the use of nuclear energy since the events *proved*—to them at least—that nuclear plant designers were incapable of building safe facilities that could withstand every possible force that nature (or terrorists) might throw.

Antinuclear Activism Is Based on Misinformation

During the public hearings held last week [December 2011] by the House Oversight Committee and the Senate Committee on the Environment and Public Works, questioners repeatedly introduced the topic of Fukushima and the actions we should be taking in response to that event. In fact, the Senate hearing was specifically titled *Review of the NRC's Near-Term Task Force Recommendations for Enhancing Reactor Safety in the 21st Century*.

However, it appeared to me that most of the people who brought up the topic had done little serious study to understand the full story. They appear happy to hope that no one else has done their homework either.

They did not appear to know that the four damaged units had been cooled down to a safe shutdown condition. They did not appear to understand that the water that had been contaminated was either being cleaned up by a filtering system or had been safely diluted by the bazillions of gallons of water in the Pacific Ocean.

They did not appear to realize that plans are *finally* underway to allow the forcibly displaced population to begin returning home to clean up. There is a lot of work to do to clean up both the effects of the tsunami and the artificially imposed effects on facilities and livestock populations that have not been maintained by human beings for more than nine months.

Health and Safety Risks Are Within the Acceptable Range

The people for whom "Fukushima" is a scare word designed to encourage others to abandon the beneficial use of nuclear energy did not appear to know that the "safety" levels that have been officially imposed regarding radiation exposure are so low that they will impose an added risk of contracting cancer—even using the most pessimistic assumptions and the most conservative model—of about 0.5%. That added risk is about 20–50 times less than someone might assume by smoking and about 10–20 times less than someone might assume by being obese.

They also did not appear to understand that the event that some antinuclear activists and their political friends have called the worst nuclear accident in history did not release radioactive material in a sufficient concentration to have injured or killed anyone.

A critical thinking, questioning person (like [writer and environmental activist] George Monbiot) would logically conclude that, if Fukushima Daiichi represents the worst nuclear accident in history, then we should be pursuing a rapidly expanding construction program. Compared to the risks imposed by all other energy alternatives, including the risk that would be imposed by not having sufficient quantities of reliable, affordable energy, Fukushima was not so bad. It was, in fact, a dramatic example that the risks imposed by accepting the benefits of affordable, emission-free nuclear energy are well within the "acceptable" range, even in the worst realistic conditions.

Reaction from Nuclear Energy Competition

One final aspect about Fukushima worth serious consideration and deep thinking is the response to the accident by the suppliers and speculators associated with the enterprise of supplying the same product that nuclear energy supplies. The competitors have leaped in with massive investments in ads and studies to prove that "in the wake of Fukushima" they are capable of stepping in to fill whatever voids in the power supply are caused by a lower output of nuclear energy.

The natural gas industry, in particular, is beating the drums to tell the story of its newly discovered ability to extract natural gas that is tightly bound up in large deposits of shale rock located several thousand feet below the earth's surface. What some people call "the shale storm" is being offered as a bridge to a utopian vision of a world where there is no fossil fuel and no nuclear energy being used.

It is mighty "big" of fossil fuel suppliers and alternative energy system developers to tell us all that we do not have to worry about shivering in the dark. They claim that they are quite willing and able to sell us the power that we want. Of course, since digging up more coal, pumping and refining more oil and extracting more natural gas will be costly, they expect us all to pay higher prices to encourage them to undertake that increased effort.

Since building wind turbines, solar arrays and digging geothermal wells will provide a potentially large, but completely unpredictable quantity of energy, often sourced from remote areas, we will also have to pay, through electric power rates or through taxes or both, to build additional grid capacity. There are other commercial enterprises standing by to provide the additional equipment and labor required—at a price with sufficient profit margins to encourage a prompt response.

The speculators are also telling investors that it is time to buy into natural gas stocks, coal mining stocks, and alternative energy system producers because it is inevitable that those will all benefit as society turns away from nuclear energy and slows down the nuclear power plant building revival that was expected to occur before the accident.

Time to Move Forward with Nuclear Energy

Do you think that it is remotely possible that the hype, attention and repetition about the tragedy and the lack of serious discussion about the actual results has been motivated by the financial interests of the people who benefit when people decide that nuclear energy is too scary? Do you think there is even the remotest possibility that we have all be lied to, through commission and omission, about the actual risk of nuclear energy in comparison to its competitors? Are people making decisions and forming opinions based on information that has been purposely slanted against nuclear energy in order to make already rich petroleum pushers even richer?

Should you really be afraid, or should you take a hard look at the situation, at the motivations, and at the real aftermath to determine that, if Fukushima represents the worst nuclear accident in history, it is time to move forward with all due haste to replace as much of our fossil fuel burning, CO_2 generating, politically destabilizing industrial infrastructure as we can.

Please reflect deeply and identify the groups that are most logically the ones that are the most threatened by that proposition. If you decide to become an atomic energy advocate, please understand that there will be A LOT of well financed and organized opposition to even considering the possibility of turning from a hydrocarbon based economy to one that runs on uranium, thorium and plutonium.

Note

1. "Fukushima" refers to the series of natural disasters and nuclear reactor meltdowns on March 11, 2011, which destroyed the nuclear power plant in Fukushima, Japan.

> *"Nuclear power is never 'safe.' Splitting atoms to produce heat, boil water, and generate electricity is an inherently dangerous activity."*

The Fukushima Disaster Proves That Nuclear Power Risks Are Unmanageable

Jim Riccio

In the following viewpoint Jim Riccio argues that nuclear power always carries with it the risk of a meltdown with devastating consequences. The Fukushima disaster, Riccio maintains, has proven that any risk assessment claiming that certain events are "improbable" does not mean they are impossible. After all, he argues, the Fukushima disaster was caused by the "improbable" double trouble of an earthquake followed by a tsunami. Ignoring such flawed risk assessment, Riccio claims, government safety regulators have allowed safety standards to be compromised to cater to corporate interests. Riccio is a nuclear policy analyst for Greenpeace.

As you read, consider the following questions:

1. According to the author, what is atomic hubris?

Jim Riccio, "Fukushima Disaster Shows Nuclear Power Is Never 'Safe,'" *U.S. News & World Report*, July 1, 2011.

2. What percent of risk-significant accident scenarios are not modeled in nuclear risk assessments, according to the viewpoint?
3. Why has the public been exposed to greater risk and the nuclear industry to less regulation, according to Riccio?

The ongoing [March 2011] nuclear disaster at the Fukushima nuclear plant will be delivering up many lessons to those willing to listen. More than three months after the earthquake, tsunami, and subsequent meltdown of three nuclear reactors, TEPCO, the nuclear corporation that owns the plant, is no closer to controlling the meltdowns or securing twenty years of radioactive material at risk in the waste pool. A few things, however, are becoming clear.

Nuclear Power Is Never Safe

Nuclear power is never "safe." Splitting atoms to produce heat, boil water, and generate electricity is an inherently dangerous activity. Splitting atoms can be made less dangerous, but it can never be "safe." The 104 nuclear power plants in the United States and the 440 operating around the world all carry the threat of a catastrophic meltdown with devastating consequences. To claim this technology is safe is no more than atomic hubris. Nuclear power plants will fail, and when they do, the consequences are catastrophic for individuals and society. As the codiscoverer of the DNA molecule once put it, "the idea that the atom is safe is just a public relations trick."

Fukushima has reminded us, too, that probability will not protect the public from nuclear meltdowns. Long before the disaster at Fukushima, I recommended that U.S. nuclear regulators read Nassim Nicholas Taleb's *The Black Swan*. Taleb addresses the impact of low-probability, high-consequence events such as Fukushima and points out the psychological trap of relying on probability to protect us. Taleb has intentionally avoided doing interviews on the Fukushima fiasco, but wrote:

> I spent the last two decades explaining . . . why we should not talk about small probabilities in any domain. Science cannot deal with them. It is irresponsible to talk about small probabilities and make people rely on them, except for natural systems that have been standing for 3 billion years (not manmade ones for which the probabilities are derived theoretically, such as the nuclear field for which the effective track record is only 60 years).

Probability provides cold comfort when reactors are overwhelmed by forces they were never designed to resist—such as the meltdown of the radioactive fuel rods that make up the core of the nuclear reactor. But the nuclear industry and its regulators have been doing precisely what Taleb warns against.

As has been well documented by the Associated Press, the *New York Times*, *Huffington Post*, ProPublica, and others, the Nuclear Regulatory Commission, or NRC, has been captured by the nuclear industry and has been in regulatory retreat for over a decade. At the behest of the industry, the NRC has been busy deregulating safety standards based on the probability that the Black Swan, i.e., a meltdown, will not occur. Sadly, these same regulators have ignored the flaws in their risk assessments. According to NRC documents, between 42 percent and 59 percent of the most risk-significant accident scenarios aren't even modeled in nuclear risk assessments. The NRC and the nuclear industry have relied on risk models that leave them half blind to the very events they're attempting to avoid.

Corporate Profit Outweighs Public Safety

Despite recognized flaws in their risk assessments, government regulators have allowed the nuclear industry to whittle away at regulations intended to protect the public in order to reduce the cost of producing electricity with nuclear reactors. As a result, safety has been compromised. The nuclear bureaucrats have lost

The Fukushima Disaster Is "The Worst on Its Scale"

Thomas Breuer, Head of the Climate and Energy Unit at Greenpeace, said in a written statement: "The (nuclear) industry both inside and outside Japan have again been underplaying the human consequences of this terrible tragedy [the March 11, 2011 nuclear meltdowns at the Fukushima Nuclear power plant], and only now after a month has this disaster been accepted for what it is—the worst on its scale."

Thair Shaikh, "Q & A: Is Fukushima as Bad as Chernobyl?," CNN World, April 12, 2011.

sight of their safety mission and instead have weakened nuclear plant regulations to allow reactors to run longer and harder than ever before. Government officials have repeatedly placed corporate profit ahead of public safety. In order to increase the corporate bottom line, the public has been exposed to greater risk while the industry is exposed to less regulation. All the while, these corporations and captured regulators claim splitting atoms on a shoestring is "safe."

As we saw at Three Mile Island,[1] Chernobyl,[2] and now Fukushima, nuclear power is never "safe." The improbable happens, and regulations put in place by nuclear bureaucrats are insufficient to the catastrophe. Probability will not protect the public from the consequences of a nuclear meltdown. The nuclear industry's practice of lulling regulators into complacency based on low probability of a meltdown is irresponsible at the least. Rather than promoting the expanded use of nuclear power, government regulators will be lucky if they can manage the end of the nuclear age and secure deadly radioactive wastes without more Black Swan events like the fiasco at Fukushima.

Notes

1. On March 28, 1979, mechanical failures caused a nuclear meltdown at the Three Mile Island nuclear power plant in Pennsylvania.
2. On April 26, 1986, an explosion and fire caused a major meltdown at the Chernobyl Nuclear Power Plant in Ukraine, then part of the Soviet Union.

Viewpoint 3

> *"It is now clear that no one need fear a potential public health catastrophe simply because a fuel meltdown happens."*

The Risks of Nuclear Accidents or Terrorist Attacks on Plants Are Minimal and Manageable

World Nuclear Association

In the following viewpoint the World Nuclear Association argues that the nuclear industry has been successful in avoiding major accidents. Only three accidents—at Chernobyl, Three Mile Island and Fukushima—have occurred in more than fifty years, resulting in less severe consequences than feared, according to the association. Accidents such as the meltdown at Fukushima, the association maintains, will lead to continuous safety improvements in reactor design, operational safety, and accident management. The association also claims that current reactor design can withstand most natural disasters and terrorist attacks. Strict oversight and international collaboration make nuclear power safer than any other form of energy production, the association concludes. The World Nuclear Association promotes nuclear power and supports companies in the industry.

Edited from World Nuclear Association information paper "Safety of Nuclear Power Reactors," March 2012. www.world-nuclear.org/info/inf06.html.

As you read, consider the following questions:

1. What were the three major nuclear accidents, according to the viewpoint?
2. What are the key aspects of the "defence-in-depth" approach, as explained in the viewpoint?
3. What changes does the viewpoint state were made to the Nuclear Regulatory Commissions' security requirements after the 9/11 terrorist attacks?

In the 1950s attention turned to harnessing the power of the atom in a controlled way, as demonstrated [by the] Chicago [Pile-1 (CP-1), the world's first man-made nuclear reactor] in 1942 and subsequently for military research, and applying the steady heat yield to generate electricity. This naturally gave rise to concerns about accidents and their possible effects. However, with nuclear power, safety depends on much the same factors as in any comparable industry: intelligent planning, proper design with conservative margins and back-up systems, high-quality components and a well-developed safety culture in operations.

The Nuclear Industry Has Successfully Avoided Accidents

A particular nuclear scenario was loss of cooling which resulted in melting of the nuclear reactor core, and this motivated studies on both the physical and chemical possibilities as well as the biological effects of any dispersed radioactivity. Those responsible for nuclear power technology in the West devoted extraordinary effort to ensuring that a meltdown of the reactor core would not take place, since it was assumed that a meltdown of the core would create a major public hazard, and if uncontained, a tragic accident with likely multiple fatalities.

In avoiding such accidents, the industry has been very successful. In over 14,500 cumulative reactor-years of commercial operation in 32 countries, there have been only three major accidents to nuclear power plants—Three Mile Island [on March 28, 1979, in Pennsylvania], Chernobyl, [on April 26, 1986, in the Ukraine] and Fukushima [on March 11, 2011, in Japan]—the second being of little relevance to reactor design outside the old Soviet bloc.

An Accident Is Unlikely to Cause Dramatic Harm

It was not until the late 1970s that detailed analyses and large-scale testing, followed by the 1979 meltdown of the Three Mile Island reactor, began to make clear that even the worst possible accident in a conventional western nuclear power plant or its fuel would not be likely to cause dramatic public harm. The industry still works hard to minimize the probability of a meltdown accident, but it is now clear that no one need fear a potential public health catastrophe simply because a fuel meltdown happens. Fukushima has made that clear, with a triple meltdown causing no fatalities or serious radiation doses to anyone, while over two hundred people continued working on the site to mitigate the accident's effects.

The decades-long test and analysis program showed that less radioactivity escapes from molten fuel than initially assumed, and that most of this radioactive material is not readily mobilized beyond the immediate internal structure. Thus, even if the containment structure that surrounds all modern nuclear plants were ruptured, as it has been with at least one of the Fukushima reactors, it is still very effective in preventing escape of most radioactivity. . . .

Of all the accidents and incidents, only the Chernobyl and Fukushima accidents resulted in radiation doses to the public greater than those resulting from the exposure to natural sources. The Fukushima accident resulted in some radiation exposure of workers at the plant, but not such as to threaten their health, unlike Chernobyl. Other incidents (and one "accident") have been completely confined to the plant.

Apart from Chernobyl, no nuclear workers or members of the public have ever died as a result of exposure to radiation due to a commercial nuclear reactor incident. Most of the serious radiological injuries and deaths that occur each year (2–4 deaths and many more exposures above regulatory limits) are the result of large uncontrolled radiation sources, such as abandoned medical or industrial equipment. . . .

It should be emphasised that a commercial-type power reactor simply cannot under any circumstances explode like a nuclear bomb—the fuel is not enriched beyond about 5%.

We Can Learn from Accidents

The International Atomic Energy Agency (IAEA) was set up by the United Nations in 1957. One of its functions was to act as an auditor of world nuclear safety, and this role was increased greatly following the Chernobyl accident. It prescribes safety procedures and the reporting of even minor incidents. Its role has been strengthened since 1996. Every country which operates nuclear power plants has a nuclear safety inspectorate and all of these work closely with the IAEA.

While nuclear power plants are designed to be safe in their operation and safe in the event of any malfunction or accident, no industrial activity can be represented as entirely risk-free. Incidents and accidents may happen, and as in other industries, will lead to progressive improvement in safety. . . .

The main safety concern has always been the possibility of an uncontrolled release of radioactive material, leading to contamination and consequent radiation exposure off-site. Earlier assumptions were that this would be likely in the event of a major loss of cooling accident (LOCA) which resulted in a core melt. The TMI [Three Mile Island] experience suggested otherwise, but at Fukushima this is exactly what happened. In the light of better understanding of the physics and chemistry of material in a reactor core under extreme conditions it became evident that even a severe core melt coupled with breach of containment would be unlikely to create a major radiological disaster from many Western reactor designs, but the Fukushima accident showed that this did not apply to all. Studies of the post-accident situation at Three Mile Island (where there was no breach of containment) supported the suggestion, and analysis of Fukushima is pending.

Certainly the matter was severely tested with three reactors of the Fukushima Daiichi nuclear power plant in Japan in March 2011. Cooling was lost after a shutdown, and it proved impossible to restore it sufficiently to prevent severe damage to the fuel. The reactors, dating from 1971–75, were written off. A fourth is also written off due to damage from a hydrogen explosion. . . .

Nuclear Accidents Are Less Severe than Other Industrial Accidents

It has long been asserted that nuclear reactor accidents are the epitome of low-probability but high-consequence risks. Understandably, with this in mind, some people were disinclined to accept the risk, however low the probability. However, the physics and chemistry of a reactor core, coupled with but not wholly depending on the engineering, mean that the consequences of an accident are likely in fact to be much less severe than those from other industrial and energy sources. Experience, including Fukushima, bears this out. . . .

The use of nuclear energy for electricity generation can be considered extremely safe. Every year several thousand people die in coal mines to provide this widely used fuel for electricity. There are also significant health and environmental effects arising from fossil fuel use. To date, even the Fukushima accident has caused no deaths, and the IAEA reported on 1 June 2011: "to date, no health effects have been reported in any person as a result of radiation exposure." . . .

Defence-in-Depth Achieves Maximum Security

To achieve optimum safety, nuclear plants in the western world operate using a *"defence-in-depth" approach*, with multiple safety systems supplementing the natural features of the reactor core. Key aspects of the approach are:

- high-quality design and construction,
- equipment which prevents operational disturbances or human failures and errors developing into problems,
- comprehensive monitoring and regular testing to detect equipment or operator failures,
- redundant and diverse systems to control damage to the fuel and prevent significant radioactive releases,
- provision to confine the effects of severe fuel damage (or any other problem) to the plant itself.

These can be summed up as: Prevention, Monitoring, and Action (to mitigate consequences of failures). . . .

Traditional reactor safety systems are "active" in the sense that they involve electrical or mechanical operation on command. Some engineered systems operate passively, e.g. pressure relief valves. Both require parallel redundant systems. Inherent or full passive safety design depends only on physical phenomena such as convection, gravity or resistance to high temperatures, not on functioning of engineered components. All reactors have some elements of inherent safety as mentioned above, but in some recent designs the passive or inherent features substitute for active systems in cooling etc. Such a design would have averted the Fukushima accident, where loss of electrical power resulted in loss of cooling function.

The basis of design assumes a threat where due to accident or malign intent (e.g. terrorism) there is core melting and a breach of containment. This double possibility has been well studied and provides the basis of exclusion zones and contingency plans. Apparently during the Cold War neither Russia nor the USA targeted the other's nuclear power plants because the likely damage would be modest.

Nuclear power plants are designed with sensors to shut them down automatically in an earthquake, and this is a vital consideration in many parts of the world. . . .

The Defence-in-Depth Approach

Defence-in-depth consists . . . of different levels of equipment and procedures in order to maintain the effectiveness of physical barriers placed between radioactive materials and workers, the public, or the environment—in normal operation—anticipated operational occurrences and, for some barriers, in accidents at the plant. Defence-in-depth is implemented through design and operation to provide a graded protection against a wide variety of transients, incidents, and accidents, including equipment failures and human errors within the plant and events initiated outside the plant. . . .

[The] defence-in-depth concept [is] centred on several levels of protection, including successive barriers preventing the release of radioactive material to the environment. The objectives are as follows:

- to compensate for potential human and component failures;
- to maintain the effectiveness of the barriers by averting damage to the plant and to the barriers themselves; and
- to protect the public and the environment from harm in the event that these barriers are not fully effective.

International Nuclear Safety Advisory Group, "Defence in Depth in Nuclear Safety," International Atomic Energy Agency, 1996. www-pub.iaea.org.

At Fukushima Daiichi in March 2011 the three operating reactors shut down automatically, and were being cooled as designed by the normal residual heat removal system using power from the back-up generators, until the tsunami swamped them an hour later. The emergency core cooling systems then failed.

Days later, a separate problem emerged as spent fuel ponds lost water. Full analysis of the accident is pending, but it is likely that the results will include more attention being given to siting criteria and the design of back-up power and cooling, as well as emergency management procedures.

Nuclear plants have Severe Accident Mitigation Guidelines (SAMG, or in Japan: SAG), and most of these, including all those in the USA, address what should be done for accidents beyond design basis, and where several systems may be disabled. . . .

European "Stress Tests" Following the Fukushima Accident

Assessment of the aspects of nuclear plant safety highlighted by the Fukushima accident is being applied to the 143 nuclear reactors in the EU's 27 member states, as well as those in any neighbouring states that have decided to take part. These so-called "stress tests" involved targeted reassessment of each power reactor's safety margins in the light of extreme natural events such as earthquakes and flooding . . . as well as on loss of safety functions and severe accident management following any initiating event. . . .

The results of the reassessment will be peer-reviewed and shared among regulators. They may indicate a need for additional technical or organisational safety provisions. WENRA [Western European Nuclear Regulators Association] noted that it remains a national responsibility to take any appropriate measures resulting from the reassessment. . . .

Severe Accident Management

In addition to engineering and procedures which reduce the risk and severity of accidents, all plants have guidelines for Severe Accident Management or Mitigation (SAM). These conspicuously came into play after the Fukushima accident, where staff had immense challenges in the absence of power and with disabled cooling systems following damage done by the tsunami.

The experience following that accident is being applied not only in design but also in such guidelines, and peer reviews on nuclear plants will focus more on these than previously.

In mid 2011 the IAEA Incident and Emergency Centre launched a new secure web-based communications platform to unify and simplify information exchange during nuclear or radiological emergencies. The Unified System for Information Exchange on Incidents and Emergencies (USIE) has been under development since 2009 but was actually launched during the emergency response to the accident at Fukushima. . . .

International Collaboration to Improve Safety

There is a great deal of international cooperation on nuclear safety issues, in particular the exchange of operating experience under the auspices of the World Association of Nuclear Operators (WANO) which was set up in 1989. In practical terms this is the most effective international means of achieving very high levels of safety through its four major programs: peer reviews; operating experience; technical support and exchange; and professional and technical development. WANO peer reviews are the main proactive way of sharing experience and expertise, and by the end of 2009 every one of the world's commercial nuclear power plants had been peer-reviewed at least once. Following the Fukushima accident these have been stepped up to one every four years at each plant, with follow-up visits in between, and the scope extended from operational safety to include plant design upgrades. Pre-startup reviews of new plants are being increased.

The IAEA Convention on Nuclear Safety (CNS) was drawn up during a series of expert level meetings from 1992 to 1994 and was the result of considerable work by Governments, national nuclear safety authorities and the IAEA Secretariat. Its aim is to legally commit participating States operating land-based nuclear power plants to maintain a high level of safety by setting international benchmarks to which States would subscribe. . . .

The Convention entered into force in October 1996. As of September 2009, there were 79 signatories to the Convention, 66 of which are contracting parties, including all countries with operating nuclear power plants. . . .

Problems with Ageing Nuclear Plants

Several issues arise in prolonging the lives of nuclear plants which were originally designed for 30 or 40-year operating lives. Systems, structures and components (SSC) whose characteristics change gradually with time or use are the subject of attention.

Some components simply wear out, corrode or degrade to a low level of efficiency. These need to be replaced. Steam generators are the most prominent and expensive of these, and many have been replaced after about 30 years where the reactor otherwise has the prospect of running for 60 years. This is essentially an economic decision. Lesser components are more straightforward to replace as they age, and some may be safety-related as well as economic. In Candu [Canadian pressurized heavy water] reactors, pressure tube replacement has been undertaken on some older plants, after some 30 years of operation.

A second issue is that of obsolescence. For instance, older reactors have analogue instrument and control systems, and a question must be faced regarding whether these are replaced with digital in a major mid-life overhaul, or simply maintained.

Thirdly, the properties of materials may degrade with age, particularly with heat and neutron irradiation. In some early Russian pressurized water reactors, the pressure vessel is relatively narrow and is thus subject to greater neutron bombardment than a wider one. This raises questions of embrittlement, and has had to be checked carefully before extending licences.

In respect to all these aspects, periodic safety reviews are undertaken on older plants in line with the IAEA safety convention and WANO's [World Association of Nuclear Operators] safety culture principles to ensure that safety margins are maintained. . . .

In the USA most of the more than one hundred reactors are expected to be granted licence extensions from 40 to 60 years. This justifies significant capital expenditure in upgrading systems and components, including building in extra performance margins. There is widespread agreement that further extensions may be justified, and this prospect is driving research on ageing to ensure both safety and reliability in older plants. . . .

Nuclear Plants Can Withstand Acts of Terrorism

Since the World Trade Centre attacks in New York in 2001 there has been concern about the consequences of a large aircraft being used to attack a nuclear facility with the purpose of releasing radioactive materials. Various studies have looked at similar attacks on nuclear power plants. They show that nuclear reactors would be more resistant to such attacks than virtually any other civil installations. A thorough study was undertaken by the US Electric Power Research Institute (EPRI) using specialist consultants and paid for by the US Dept. of Energy. It concludes that US reactor structures "are robust and (would) protect the fuel from impacts of large commercial aircraft". . . .

Looking at spent fuel storage pools, similar analyses showed no breach. Dry storage and transport casks retained their integrity. "There would be no release of radionuclides to the environment".

Similarly, the massive structures mean that any terrorist attack even inside a plant (which are well defended) and causing loss of cooling, core melting and breach of containment would not result in any significant radioactive releases.

However, while the main structures are robust, the 2001 attacks did lead to increased security requirements and plants were required by NRC [Nuclear Regulatory Commission] to install barriers, bulletproof security stations and other physical modifications which in the USA are estimated by the industry association to have cost some $2 billion across the country. . . .

Nuclear Reactor Operation Is Safer than Generating Coal-Based Power

The designs for nuclear plants being developed for implementation in coming decades contain numerous safety improvements based on operational experience. The first two of these advanced reactors began operating in Japan in 1996.

One major feature they have in common (beyond safety engineering already standard in Western reactors) is passive safety systems, requiring no operator intervention in the event of a major malfunction. . . .

Many occupational accident statistics have been generated over the last 40 years of nuclear reactor operations in the US and UK. These can be compared with those from coal-fired power generation. All show that nuclear is a distinctly safer way to produce electricity.

Viewpoint 

> *"There have been 57 accidents since the Chernobyl disaster in 1986 . . . [that] collectively killed more people than have died in commercial US airline accidents since 1982."*

Nuclear Accidents Are Common and Pose Inevitable Safety Risks

Benjamin K. Sovacool

In the following viewpoint Benjamin K. Sovacool argues that serious nuclear accidents may be rare, but incidents at nuclear power plants and other facilities related to nuclear power processing are common, collectively causing more fatalities and property damage than other power sources. Given that even a single serious accident could cause unmanageable damage, Sovacool asserts, nuclear power is not a safe, clean, or reliable alternative to other power sources. Sovacool is a professor of public policy at the University of Singapore and has published books and articles on nuclear power.

As you read, consider the following questions:

1. What are "incidents" and "accidents," according to Sovacool?

Benjamin K. Sovacool, "The Dirt on Nuclear Power," *Project Syndicate*, March 16, 2011. www.projectsyndicate.org.

2. What does Sovacool say that the August 2003 blackout revealed?
3. According to the author, does the historical record show that nuclear power is safe?

Japan's nuclear crisis [the Fukushima nuclear reactor meltdown on March 11, 2011] is a nightmare, but it is not an anomaly. In fact, it is only the latest in a long line of nuclear accidents involving meltdowns, explosions, fires, and loss of coolant—accidents that have occurred during both normal operation and emergency conditions, such as droughts and earthquakes.

Costly Nuclear Incidents and Accidents Are Common

Nuclear safety demands clarity about terms. The Nuclear Regulatory Commission in the United States generally separates unplanned nuclear "events" into two classes, "incidents" and "accidents." Incidents are unforeseen events and technical failures that occur during normal plant operation and result in no off-site releases of radiation or severe damage to equipment. Accidents refer to either off-site releases of radiation or severe damage to plant equipment.

The International Nuclear and Radiological Event Scale uses a seven-level ranking scheme to rate the significance of nuclear and radiological events: levels 1–3 are "incidents," and 4–7 are "accidents," with a "Level 7 Major Accident" consisting of "a major release of radioactive material with widespread health and environmental effects requiring implementation of planned and extended countermeasures."

Under these classifications, the number of nuclear accidents, even including the meltdowns at Fukushima Daiichi and Fukushima Daini, is low. But if one redefines an accident to include incidents that either resulted in the loss of human life or more than $50,000 in property damage, a very different picture emerges.

At least 99 nuclear accidents meeting this definition, totaling more than $20.5 billion in damages, occurred worldwide from 1952 to 2009—or more than one incident and $330 million in damage every year, on average, for the past three decades. And, of course, this average does not include the Fukushima catastrophe.

Indeed, when compared to other energy sources, nuclear power ranks higher than oil, coal, and natural gas systems in terms of fatalities, second only to hydroelectric dams. There have been 57 accidents since the Chernobyl disaster in 1986.[1] While only a few involved fatalities, those that did collectively killed more people than have died in commercial US airline accidents since 1982.

Another index of nuclear-power accidents—this one including costs beyond death and property damage, such as injured or irradiated workers and malfunctions that did not result in shutdowns or leaks—documented 956 incidents from 1942 to 2007. And yet another documented more than 30,000 mishaps at US nuclear-power plants alone, many with the potential to have caused serious meltdowns, between the 1979 accident at Three Mile Island in Pennsylvania and 2009.

Dangerous Nuclear Incidents and Accidents Are Not Limited to Reactor Sites

Mistakes are not limited to reactor sites. Accidents at the Savannah River reprocessing plant released ten times as much radioiodine as the accident at Three Mile Island, and a fire at the Gulf United facility in New York in 1972 scattered an undisclosed amount of plutonium, forcing the plant to shut down permanently.

At the Mayak Industrial Reprocessing Complex in Russia's southern Urals, a storage tank holding nitrate acetate salts exploded in 1957, releasing a massive amount of radioactive material over 20,000 square kilometers, forcing the evacuation of 272,000 people. In September 1994, an explosion at Indonesia's

Serrong research reactor was triggered by the ignition of methane gas that had seeped from a storage room and exploded when a worker lit a cigarette.

Accidents have also occurred when nuclear reactors are shut down for refueling or to move spent nuclear fuel into storage. In 1999, operators loading spent fuel into dry-storage at the Trojan Reactor in Oregon found that the protective zinc-carbon coating had started to produce hydrogen, which caused a small explosion.

Unfortunately, on-site accidents at nuclear reactors and fuel facilities are not the only cause of concern. The August 2003 blackout in the northeastern US revealed that more than a dozen nuclear reactors in the US and Canada were not properly maintaining backup diesel generators. In Ontario during the blackout, reactors designed to unlink from the grid automatically and remain in standby mode instead went into full shutdown, with only two of twelve reactors behaving as expected.

As environmental lawyers Richard Webster and Julie LeMense argued in 2008, "the nuclear industry . . . is like the financial industry was prior to the crisis" that erupted that year. "[T]here are many risks that are not being properly managed or regulated."

A Single Serious Accident Poses Unmanageable Risks

This state of affairs is worrying, to say the least, given the severity of harm that a single serious accident can cause. The meltdown of a 500-megawatt reactor located 30 miles from a city would cause the immediate death of an estimated 45,000 people, injure roughly another 70,000, and cause $17 billion in property damage.

A successful attack or accident at the Indian Point power plant near New York City, apparently part of Al Qaeda's plan for [the attacks on] September 11, 2001, would have resulted in 43,700 immediate fatalities and 518,000 cancer deaths, with cleanup costs reaching $2 trillion.

To put a serious accident in context, according to data from my . . . book *Contesting the Future of Nuclear Power*, if 10 million people were exposed to radiation from a complete nuclear meltdown (the containment structures fail completely, exposing the inner reactor core to air), about 100,000 would die from acute radiation sickness within six weeks. About 50,000 would experience acute breathlessness, and 240,000 would develop acute hypothyroidism. About 350,000 males would be temporarily sterile, 100,000 women would stop menstruating, and 100,000 children would be born with cognitive deficiencies. There would be thousands of spontaneous abortions and more than 300,000 later cancers.

Advocates of nuclear energy have made considerable political headway around the world in recent years, touting it as a safe, clean, and reliable alternative to fossil fuels. But the historical record clearly shows otherwise. Perhaps the unfolding tragedy in Japan will finally be enough to stop the nuclear renaissance from materializing.

Note

1. On April 26, 1986, an explosion and fire at the Chernobyl Nuclear Power Plant in Ukraine caused radioactive contamination that spread over the western part of the Soviet Union and Europe.

> *"For nuclear energy to expand, the public must trust the nuclear industry. . . . It must trust reactor designers to create new reactors that do not share the vulnerabilities of older ones."*

Better Design and Oversight Will Safeguard Nuclear Plants Against Natural Disasters and Terrorism

James M. Acton

In the following viewpoint James M. Acton argues that the current approach to safety at nuclear plants—"defense in depth"—is flawed, because backup systems can be wiped out by a single event, such as the earthquake and tsunami in Fukushima. A firm supporter of nuclear power, Acton calls for a reassessment of the current design of nuclear reactors and argues that new plants with enhanced safety features are needed to regain the public's trust in nuclear power. Acton, a physicist, is an associate in the Nuclear Policy Program at the Carnegie Endowment for International Peace.

James M. Acton, "Nuclear Power Is Worth the Risk," *Foreign Policy*, March 14, 2011.

As you read, consider the following questions:

1. What is meant by "defense in depth" according to Acton?
2. What does Acton say was swamped by the tsunami at Fukushima?
3. According to the author, why will the nuclear industry resist a reassessment of the design basis for nuclear plants?

Until March 11 [2011], with the 25th anniversary of the Chernobyl accident [the April 26, 1986, explosion and meltdown at a nuclear power plant in the Ukraine] approaching—and memories of that disaster receding—safety concerns no longer appeared to be the killer argument against nuclear power they once were. Instead, another fear—of climate change—looked like it might be driving a "nuclear renaissance" as states sought carbon-free energy sources. But the ongoing crisis at Japan's Fukushima Daiichi Nuclear Power Station [a meltdown brought on by an earthquake and tsunami on March 11, 2011] will return safety to the forefront of the nuclear power debate. Even the most ardent industry advocates now recognize that the unfolding crisis inside two reactors there—shown on live television and beamed around the world—has left the future of their industry in doubt.

Nevertheless, the case for nuclear power remains strong. All forms of energy generation carry risks. Fossil fuels, which (for the time being at least) are nuclear energy's principal rival, carry the risk of catastrophic climate change. And as we're seeing in Japan, we haven't eliminated all the dangers associated with nuclear power, even though accidents are few and far between.

The Current Approach to Safety Is Flawed

Good public policy involves balancing these risks. Persuading the public to accept the risks of nuclear energy will, however, not be easy. To do so, the nuclear industry will have to resist a strong temptation to argue that the accident in Japan was simply an extraordinarily improbable confluence of events, and that everything is just fine. Instead, it must recognize and correct the deficiencies of its current approach to safety.

When it comes to safety, the nuclear industry emphasizes the concept of "defense in depth." Reactors are designed with layers of redundant safety systems. There's the main cooling system, a backup to it, a backup to the backup, a backup to the backup to the backup, and so on. A major accident can only occur if all these systems fail simultaneously. By adding extra layers of redundancy, the probability of such a catastrophic failure can—in theory at least—be made too small to worry about.

Defense in depth is a good idea. But it suffers from one fundamental flaw: the possibility that a disaster might knock out all of the backup systems. A reactor can have as many layers of defense as you like, but if they can all be disabled by a single event, then redundancy adds much less to safety than might first meet the eye.

When the Backup Plan Fails

This kind of failure occurred at Fukushima Daiichi on March 11 [2011]. As soon as the earthquake struck, the reactors scrammed: The control rods, used to modulate the speed of the nuclear reaction, were inserted into the reactor cores, shutting off the nuclear reactions. So far so good. Nevertheless, the cores were still hot and needed to be cooled. This in turn required electricity in order to power the pumps, which bring in water to cool the fuel.

Unfortunately, one of the external power lines that was designed to provide electricity in just such a contingency was itself disrupted by the earthquake. This shouldn't have mattered because there was a backup. But, according to a news release issued by the power-plant operator, the malfunction in one external supply somehow caused off-site power to be lost entirely.

Once again, this shouldn't have been too much of an issue. There was a backup to the backup in the form of on-site diesel

Why the Public Lost Trust in Nuclear Power

Worries about major accidents and radioactive waste storage, the invisible effects of radiation, and distrust brought on by the early secrecy and hubris of the nuclear industry, all combined in a lethal cocktail which very quickly served to stigmatise civilian nuclear power.

"A Shift in Public Attitudes to Nuclear Power," Channel 4 News, March 17, 2011. www.channel4.com.

generators. And, sure enough, they kicked in. Fifty-five minutes later, however, they were swamped by the tsunami that followed the earthquake. From that moment on, plant operators were in a desperate struggle to prevent core melting.

Japanese regulators are certainly aware of the danger of earthquakes; they take safety extremely seriously. Like other buildings in Japan, nuclear reactors must be able to withstand earthquakes. The problem, as we now know, is that there is a significant chance of them falling victim to events more extreme than those they were designed to withstand.

This problem was highlighted by the earthquake centered near the Kashiwazaki-Kariwa nuclear power plant [located in Japan; the largest power plant in the world] in 2007. The earth movements generated by that quake were larger than the plant's design limit. Fortunately, there was not a major accident; the safety systems worked as designed in spite of the quake's physical impact. Before the plant could reopen, however, new safety features had to be added to ensure that it was capable of withstanding bigger earthquakes.

Calling for a Reassessment of the Nuclear Design Basis

Of course, the issues raised by the 2007 and 2011 earthquakes are relevant to the whole world—not just Japan. What is needed now is a sober and careful assessment of what engineers call the "design basis" for all nuclear power plants worldwide—those already in operation, those under construction, and those being planned. Specifically, we need to determine whether they are truly capable of withstanding the whole range of natural and man-made disasters that might befall them, from floods to earthquakes to terrorism.

Even after the ongoing disaster in Japan, the nuclear industry is unlikely to welcome such an exercise. It is almost certain to argue that a whole-scale reassessment is unnecessary because existing standards are adequate. But after two earthquakes in less than four years shook Japanese reactors beyond their design limits, this argument is simply not credible. It is also self-defeating.

For nuclear energy to expand, the public must trust the nuclear industry. It must trust reactor operators to run their reactors safely. It must trust regulators to ensure there is adequate oversight. And, most importantly perhaps, it must trust reactor designers to create new reactors that do not share the vulnerabilities of older ones.

This last point is crucial. New reactors, with enhanced safety features, would almost certainly not have befallen the same fate as those at Fukushima Daiichi, which is four decades old. Convincing the public of this argument will be extremely hard now, however.

Safety Issues Are the Public's Top Concern

After Chernobyl, the nuclear industry argued that—as far as safety was concerned—Soviet RBMK-type reactors, like the one involved in the 1986 accident, had about as much in common with modern Western reactors as an inflatable dinghy does with an ocean liner. And they were right. But their argument made very little impact because the nuclear industry had lost the public's trust.

It is vital the nuclear industry does not make the same mistake now. It must not try to sweep safety issues under the carpet by telling people that everything is OK and that they should not worry. This strategy simply won't work. What might work is to acknowledge the problem and work to fix it.

"The Fukushima Daiichi crisis has revealed significant vulnerabilities in nuclear safety and has shaken public confidence. . . . New nuclear plants will have to be substantially safer than the current generation."

Design Changes and Increased Oversight Cannot Protect Nuclear Plants from Natural Disasters or Terrorism

Edwin Lyman

In the following viewpoint Edwin Lyman explains that small modular nuclear reactors, often considered the design choice of the future, are not safer and are more expensive than larger nuclear plants. Cutting costs by weakening regulatory requirements for smaller plants makes them more vulnerable to natural disasters and terrorist attacks, Lyman maintains. Lyman concludes that the Fukushima disaster has shown that significant safety margins ("the gold standard") have to remain intact for all reactors to prevent serious nuclear accidents. Lyman is a senior staff scientist in the Global Security program at the Union of Concerned Scientists in Washington, DC.

Edwin Lyman, "An Examination of the Safety and Economics of Light Water Small Modular Reactors," Testimony before the Energy and Water Subcommittee, Committee of Appropriations, US Senate, July 14, 2011.

As you read, consider the following questions:

1. Which claims by proponents of small modular reactors does the author find unpersuasive?
2. How is the industry for small modular reactors attempting to cut costs, according to Lyman?
3. What, according to the viewpoint, are the prerequisites for safe deployment of small nuclear reactors?

The Union of Concerned Scientists [UCS] is neither pro- nor anti-nuclear power, but has served as a nuclear power safety and security watchdog for over forty years. UCS is also deeply concerned about global climate change and has not ruled out an expansion of nuclear power as an option to help reduce greenhouse gas emissions—provided that it is affordable relative to other low-carbon options and that it meets very high standards of safety and security. However, the Fukushima Daiichi crisis [the meltdown following an earthquake and tsunami on March 11, 2011] has revealed significant vulnerabilities in nuclear safety and has shaken public confidence in nuclear power. If we want to reduce the risk of another Fukushima in the future, new nuclear plants will have to be substantially safer than the current generation. To this end, we believe that the nuclear industry and the Energy Department should work together to focus on developing safer nuclear plant designs, and that Congress should direct the Energy Department to spend taxpayer money only on support of technologies that have the potential to provide significantly greater levels of safety and security than currently operating reactors. The nuclear industry will have to work hard to regain the public trust.

Small Modular Reactors Are Not Safer than Large Reactors

Proponents of small modular reactors (SMRs) claim that their designs have inherent safety features compared to large reactors, and some even argue that their reactors would have been able to withstand an event as severe as Fukushima. We find these claims to be unpersuasive. For any plant, large or small, the key factor is the most severe event that the plant is designed to withstand—the so-called maximum "design-basis" event. Unless nuclear safety requirements for new reactors are significantly strengthened, one cannot expect that either small or large reactors will be able to survive a beyond-design-basis event like Fukushima. Although some light-water SMR concepts may have desirable safety characteristics, unless they are carefully designed, licensed, deployed and inspected, SMRs could pose comparable or even greater safety, security and proliferation risks than large reactors.

Some SMR vendors argue that their reactors will be safer because they can be built underground. While underground siting could enhance protection against certain events, such as aircraft attacks and earthquakes, it could also have disadvantages as well. For instance, emergency diesel generators and electrical switchgear at Fukushima Daiichi were installed below grade to reduce their vulnerability to seismic events, but this increased their susceptibility to flooding. And in the event of a serious accident, emergency crews could have greater difficulty accessing underground reactors.

Some SMR vendors emphasize that their designs are "passively safe." However, no credible reactor design is completely passive and can shut itself down and cool itself in every circumstance without need for intervention. Some reactor designs, large or small, have certain passive safety features that allow the reactor to depend less on operator action for a limited period of time following design-basis accidents. Small reactors may have an advantage because the lower the power of a reactor, the easier it is to cool through passive means such as natural convection cooling with water or even with air. However, accidents affecting multiple small units may cause complications that could outweigh the advantages of having lower heat removal requirements per unit. Moreover, passively safe reactors generally require some equipment, such as valves, that are designed to operate automatically but are not one hundred percent reliable.

Operators will always be needed to monitor systems to ensure they are functioning as designed, and to intervene if they fail to do so. Both passive systems and operator actions would require functioning instrumentation and control systems, which were unreliable during the severe accidents at Three Mile Island and Fukushima. Passive systems may not work as intended in the event of beyond-design-basis accidents, and as result passive designs should also be equipped with highly reliable active backup systems and associated instrumentation and control systems.

Small Modular Reactors Are More Expensive than Large Reactors

But more backup systems generally mean higher costs. This poses a particular problem for SMRs, which begin with a large economic disadvantage compared to large reactors.

According to the standard formula for economies of scale [cost reduction per unit due to increased production], the overnight capital cost per kilowatt of a 125 megawatt reactor would be roughly 2.5 times greater than that of a 1250 megawatt unit, all other factors being equal. Advocates argue that SMRs offer advantages that can offset this economic penalty, such as a better match of supply and demand, reduced up-front financing costs, reduced construction times, and an accelerated benefit from learning from the construction of multiple units. However, a 2007 paper by Westinghouse scientists and their collaborators that quantified the cost savings associated with some of these factors found that they could not overcome the size penalty: the paper found that at best, the capital cost of four 335 megawatt reactors was slightly greater than that of one 1340 megawatt reactor.

Given that there is no apparent capital cost benefit for SMRs, it is not surprising that the SMR industry is seeking to reduce operating and maintenance (O&M) costs by pressuring the Nuclear Regulatory Commission to weaken certain regulatory requirements for SMRs. Deputy Assistant Energy Secretary John Kelly

The Spread of Nuclear Equipment Cannot Be Monitored Adequately

What if a rogue government tries to take advantage of an affordable reactor to acquire nuclear expertise or materials for weapons work? Henry Sokolski, a former Pentagon official who heads the Nonproliferation Policy Education Centre, a think-tank near Washington, DC, says that Western intelligence agencies have overestimated their ability to monitor the spread of nuclear equipment and know-how. If new enrichment facilities are built to supply a slew of small nuclear reactors, materials and expertise useful in bomb-making may spread as a result.

"Thinking Small," Economist, *Technology Quarterly: Q42010, December 9, 2010. www.economist.com.*

told the Nuclear Regulatory Commission [NRC] in March that the NRC's regulatory requirements for SMRs will "directly influence the operating cost, which will be a large determinant into the economic feasibility of these plants."

Small and Large Reactors Should Follow the Same Regulatory Requirements

For example, the industry argues that regulatory requirements for SMRs in areas such as emergency planning, control room staffing and security staffing can be weakened because SMRs contain smaller quantities of radioactive substances than large reactors and therefore pose lower risks to the public. The NRC is currently considering the technical merits of these arguments.

However, small reactors will not necessarily be safer than large reactors on a per-megawatt basis. Simply put, the risk to the public posed by one 1200-megawatt reactor will be comparable to that posed by six 200-megawatt reactors (assuming that all units are independent), unless the likelihood of a serious accident is significantly lower for each small reactor. But such an outcome will not be assured under the current regulatory regime. The Nuclear Regulatory Commission has a long-standing policy that new nuclear reactors, large or small, are not required to be safer than operating reactors. One consequence of this policy is that new reactor designs that have inherent safety features not present in current reactors may not actually end up being safer in the final analysis if designers compensate by narrowing safety margins in other areas, such as by reducing containment strength or the diversity and redundancy [duplicate systems, in case one fails] of safety systems.

Any safety advantages will be eroded further if the NRC allows SMR owners to reduce emergency planning zones and the numbers of required operators and security officers.

Lessons from Fukushima: Extended Emergency Planning Zones

One of the early lessons from Fukushima is that prevention of serious nuclear accidents requires significant margins of safety to protect against extreme events. Earlier this week, UCS and the NRC's Fukushima Near-Term Task Force each issued recommendations for strengthening nuclear safety requirements. Consider the following examples:

- Emergency planning zones around U.S. nuclear plants extend to a radius of ten miles. Yet significant radiological contamination from the Fukushima accident has been detected well beyond a distance of ten miles from the plant. In fact, radiation levels high enough to trigger resettlement if they occurred in the United States have been detected over thirty miles away from the Fukushima site.

The discussion we should be having today is whether current emergency planning zones need to be increased, not whether we can shrink them for SMRs.

- As we have seen at Fukushima, nuclear plants with multiple reactors that experience severe accidents present extreme challenges. In its June 2011 report to the International Atomic Energy Agency, the Nuclear and Industrial Safety Agency of Japan (NISA) stated that:

> The accident occurred at more than one reactor at the same time, and the resources needed for accident response had to be dispersed. Moreover, as two reactors shared the facilities, the physical distance between the reactors was small. . . . The development of an accident occurring at one reactor affected the emergency responses at nearby reactors.
>
> Reflecting on the above issues, Japan will take measures to ensure that emergency operations at a reactor where an accident occurs can be conducted independently from operation at other reactors if one power station has more than one reactor. Also, Japan will assure the engineering independence of each reactor to prevent an accident at one reactor from affecting nearby reactors. In addition, Japan will promote the development of a structure that enables each unit to carry out accident responses independently, by choosing a responsible person for ensuring the nuclear safety of each unit.

- The NRC will need to consider these issues in developing its licensing approach for small modular reactor sites, which may host two to four times the number of units present at the largest U.S. nuclear plant site today. The NRC has acknowledged that some of its current regulations and procedures do not account for events affecting multiple units on a site. For instance, according to the NRC, emergency planning regulations focus on single-unit events with regard to requirements for emergency operations staffing, facilities and dose projection capability. Also, the NRC's guidance for probabilistic risk assessment, an analysis tool which is used in many regulatory applications, does not require the consideration of multiple-unit events. The NRC Fukushima Near-Term Task Force is recommending that emergency preparedness requirements be revised to address multi-unit events, which could have a significant impact on SMR licensing.

- Fukushima also demonstrated how rapidly a nuclear reactor accident can progress to a core meltdown if multiple safety systems are disabled. A well-planned and executed terrorist attack could cause damage comparable to or worse than the earthquake and tsunami that initiated the Fukushima crisis, potentially in even less time. And although Osama bin Laden is gone, the terrorist threat to domestic infrastructure may actually increase over time if al Qaeda seeks to retaliate. This is the wrong time to consider reducing security requirements for nuclear power plants, regardless of their size. However, SMR vendors have emphasized that reducing security staffing is critical for the economic viability of their projects. Christofer Mowry of B&W [nuclear power company Babcock & Silcox] told the NRC in March that "whether SMRs get deployed in large numbers or not is going to come down to O&M. And the biggest variable that we can attack directly . . . is the security issue." A Nuclear Energy Institute representative said in a presentation in June that "optimal security staffing levels [for SMRs] may appreciably differ from current levels."

Selling Small Modular Reactors Around the World Creates Difficulties for Oversight

UCS is also concerned that reducing safety and security requirements for SMRs could facilitate their sale to utilities or other entities in the United States and abroad that do not have prior experience with nuclear power. Some SMR vendors argue that their technology is so safe that it can be deployed to remote areas, military bases, and countries in the developing world that have relatively low electric demand and no nuclear experience or emergency planning infrastructure. However, SMRs deployed in this manner could raise additional safety and security concerns compared to their deployment by established and experienced nuclear utilities.

The distributed deployment of small reactors would also put great strains on existing licensing and inspection resources. Nuclear reactors are qualitatively different from other types of generating facilities, not least because they require a much more extensive safety and security inspection regime. Similarly, deployment of individual small reactors at widely distributed and remote sites around the world would strain the resources of the International Atomic Energy Agency (IAEA) and its ability to adequately safeguard reactors to guard against proliferation, since IAEA inspectors would need to visit many more locations per installed megawatt around the world. Maintaining robust oversight over vast networks of SMRs around the world would be difficult, if feasible at all.

UCS believes that SMRs are only suitable for deployment where there is an established infrastructure to cope with emergencies, and if sufficient numbers of trained operator and security staff can be provided. It is unrealistic to assume the near-term availability of SMRs that are so safe they can be shipped around the world without the need to ensure the highest levels of competence and integrity of local regulatory authorities, plant operators, emergency planning organizations and security forces. Fukushima has demonstrated the importance of timely off-site response in the event of a severe accident, so the accessibility of reactors in remote locations also must be a prime consideration. Even within the U.S., small utilities with little or no experience in operating nuclear plants need to fully appreciate the unique challenges and responsibilities associated with nuclear power, and should not expect that small modular reactors will provide any relief in this regard.

Preserving the "Gold Standard" of Safety and Oversight

UCS acknowledges the concerns of members of Congress who fear that the United States is lagging in creation of a robust SMR export market and may lose out to a country like China if it takes too long to develop and license SMRs. However, we believe that the best way for the United States to maintain a competitive edge is to establish American brands with the highest safety standards. If, as some say, NRC design certification is seen as a "gold standard" worldwide, it makes sense to preserve that standard rather than erode it by weakening SMR safety requirements.

To this end, Congress should prohibit DOE [US Department of Energy] from selecting SMR proposals for its cost-sharing program if their business case depends on a weakening of NRC safety and security regulations or marketing reactors to countries with inadequate safety rules and regulatory oversight mechanisms.

VIEWPOINT 7

> *"In low doses . . . the effects [of radiation] provide a positive stimulation to life, and may well make life-itself possible for our species."*

Minimal Exposure to Radiation Poses No Safety Risk

Leslie Corrice

In the following viewpoint, Leslie Corrice argues that the nuclear accidents at Three Mile Island and Chernobyl have proven that the "no-safe-limit theory" that originated with the aftermath of the nuclear bombs dropped on Hiroshima and Nagasaki is a myth. While there is no proof that low level radiation is dangerous, Corrice maintains, studies do prove that low level radiation can have beneficial effects. Dismissing all radiation as dangerous, Corrice concludes, blinds society to the effective uses for radiation's beneficial effects. Corrice has a degree in nuclear technology and environmental sciences and publishes The Hiroshima Syndrome, *a blog on nuclear issues.*

As you read, consider the following questions:

1. According to the "Linear No-Threshold" theory outlined in the viewpoint, which level of radiation is safe?

2. What did Paracelsus say regarding dosage, according to Corrice?
3. What, according to the author, are the positive effects of low-level radiation?

Beginning with the accident at Three Mile Island [Pennsylvania] in 1979, a widespread belief has proliferated that all levels of *ionizing radiation* are dangerous. Since 1980, *radiation hormesis* [the biological response to toxins or other stressful events] studies have shown there is actually a threshold of danger with high level exposures, but below that threshold *low dose radiation* is essentially safe and quite possibly beneficial to life. Yet this relatively new, seemingly contradictory understanding of radiation's health effects has gone essentially unknown to the general public. In order to grasp the reasons why, we must again return to the bombing of Hiroshima and Nagasaki.

The History of the No-Safe-Level Myth

The world's first atomic bomb explosion occurred on July 16, 1945, at the Alamagordo facility in New Mexico, and was called Trinity. Trinity proved that a high concentration of U-235 [uranium] and/or Pu-239 [plutonium] could be used to make a titanic explosive. Not quite a month later, an atomic bomb was dropped over Hiroshima, followed a few days later by another dropped on the outskirts of Nagasaki. Estimates of the number of Japanese killed by the initial blasts vary, but the most common numbers are 105,000 at Hiroshima and 43,000 at Nagasaki. These numbers swelled considerably by 1950 to a combined number of some 340,000 deaths. Those killed by the detonations itself and those who died days and weeks later of blast-induced physical traumas and burns, total about 200,000. This enormous number of deaths equates favorably with any explosion of more than 35 thousand tons of TNT [an explosive composed of hydrogen and nitrogroups] (35 kilotons) in urban settings of these two sizes. In addition, another 140,000 deaths occurred in the 5 years after the war which were largely attributed to the biological effects of enormous doses of Neutron and Gamma radiation from the blasts themselves and the ingested radioactive fallout the blasts produced.

Rough estimates of the radiation doses received by those who died of radiation exposure were made, and analyzed. It was discovered that doses in excess of 100 REM [unit of absorption of ionizing radiation] (Rads) inflicted over relatively short periods of time caused about a tenth of a percent of those exposed to die of a variety of radiation-related reasons, including cancer. Those who received doses in excess of ~600 REM had a 99% mortality rate. At 1000 REM, everyone died. Using these morbid statistics to graph the effects on grids which would be used for future risk estimates, a direct relationship was found between dose and death in the region between 100 REM and 1000 REM exposure. Beginning at 600 REM, the risk of dying decreased in a diminishing fashion with respect to decreasing dose. Using logarithmic graphs to keep the data analysis on one page, a straight line could be drawn from the 600 REM dose death rate of 99% and down through the 150 REM death rate of 0.1%. Though no data was used to support it, the line could be mathematically continued down to zero dose and still show potential risk of morbidity, albeit nearly zero risk at very low exposure levels. On this arbitrary line, the only zero-risk point was at zero dose.

The graph made it seem that even the tiniest imaginable doses of radiation posed a possibility of producing cancer. This fit well with the highly-conservative medical cancer-one-cell theory which held that once one cell in your body became cancerous, there was a risk of dying of that cancer. Theoretically there was no safe level of cancer, so by association there was no safe level of radiation. The "Linear No-Threshold" (LNT) or no-safe-level theory of ionizing radiation had begun. . . .

50 years ago, there was little evidence from human populations other than extrapolations (statistical predictions) to support the no-safe-level hypothesis in the low-dose range. Since it would surely overestimate rather than underestimate risk be-

low 150 REM exposures, the no-safe-level hypothesis became a paradigm of nuclear risk analysis. Little thought was given to the possible adverse psychological effect the no-safe-level hypothesis could have on the public.

Nuclear Accidents Disprove the No-Safe-Level Myth

Then came the Three Mile Island (TMI) accident in 1979, and the no-safe-level theory became widely known for the first time. Fears of a resulting cancer epidemic coursed through the effected population. Although even the most extreme estimates of radiation doses to the exposed TMI public were hundreds-to-thousands of times lower than any dose that had ever been shown to actually cause cancer, widely-published *additional* cancer estimates in the exposed population ranged from a few tens to hundreds to thousands. However, follow-up studies of cancer mortality over the thirty years after the accident have shown nothing statistically significant as a result of the accident. Remarkably, the medical records of the exposed population from Chernobyl [nuclear accident at the Chernobyl power plant in the Ukraine on April 26, 1986], some twenty-five years after the accident, also show no increases in cancer incidence or mortality. The no-safe-level hypothesis cannot account for this. If no-safe-level is correct, there should have been at least a small increase in cancer rates over the decades since TMI and Chernobyl . . . especially Chernobyl.

Astonishingly, something significant happened barely a year after TMI and went largely unreported. A research paper was published out of the University of Miami entitled *Hormesis with Ionizing Radiation* by Missouri Micro-Biology Professor T.D. Luckey. This study not only challenged the no-safe-level hypothesis, it literally disproved the hypothesis at chronic (constant) dose levels below ~five REM/year, and short term exposures as high as 50 REM. In fact, the study strongly suggested that low level "background" radiation, and all doses near background, is the operational catalyst for the immune system in mammals. No radiation exposure and the immune system doesn't work . . . a mortality rate of 100% at zero radiation dose due to massive immune system dysfunction. Thus, the study seemed to demonstrate that we cannot live without low level radiation. If there is no-safe-level to ionizing radiation because huge levels of exposure surely cause cancer, how can it be that low levels of radiation might be completely safe and possibly essential to life?

Hormesis and Radiation

Hormesis is a concept which can be traced back to the ancient Greeks, who believed that too much of anything can be deadly. Conversely, substances that are harmful in large amounts can be beneficial to life in small amounts. To put it another way, the 16th century natural philosopher Paracelsus [German-Swiss physician, 1493–1541] said, "The dose makes the poison." Surely, high doses of many substances found on Earth can be life-threatening, but low doses of the same substances often have the opposite effect. Take vitamins, for example. Typical vitamins include small concentrations of substances such as Iron, Magnesium, and Zinc, which are necessary to good health if not essential to life. In large, naturally-occurring concentrations, these minerals are deadly toxins. It seems hormesis occurs with radiation as well. Dr. Luckey discovered that doses below 50 REM produced no harmful effects at all, and there was a lethal threshold of about 100 REM.

The typical American receives about 330 millirems (.33 REM) of radiation per year from naturally radioactive atmospheric gasses, food, water, cosmic rays, the soil beneath our feet, building materials (adobe brick is a big one), and other people near us. We also get, on the average, another 30 millirems from man-made sources like medical and dental X-rays. We each get less than 1 millirem from the sum total of all nuclear power plant operations in America. The American average dose due to all sources of radiation is about 360 millirems per year, of which less than 0.3% comes from nuclear power plants. What's more, the

Will Small Radiation Doses Hurt Us?

No. Every day we live with radioactive materials around and inside our bodies as well as what is normally in our environment. However, a large dose of certain types of radiation could be harmful. That is the same answer I would give you if you asked if taking aspirin was harmful . . . yes, if you take enough of them. To put it briefly, in every medicine there is a little poison. If we use radiation safely, there are benefits. If we use radiation carelessly and high doses result, there are consequences.

Ionizing radiation can change the structure of the cells, sometimes creating potentially harmful effects that are more likely to cause changes in tissue. These changes can interfere with cellular processes so cells might not be able to divide or they might divide too much.

Although radiation has the potential to damage structures inside a cell, the structure of most concern is DNA (deoxyribonucleic acid). DNA contains the genetic information that allows each cell to function, grow, and reproduce. If DNA is damaged from radiation or some other agent (like toxic particles in smog), it has the capability to repair minor damage. However, if the damage can't be repaired or is not repaired correctly, harmful effects may occur. These effects may or may not affect how we function on a day-to-day basis. If the cells are not very important to the operation of our body, it may not matter that they have been damaged or killed. However, if the cells are in critical organs (ones that keep us alive) and a large number of the cells have been damaged or killed, that organ might not be able to function normally.

Health Physics Society, "Introduction," RadiationAnswers.org, 2007. www.radiationanswers.org.

total dose of radiation from the TMI accident to any member of the exposed public living next door to the plant and downwind was no more than 40 millirem. This means the TMI population-most-at-risk got about 400 millirems total for the year of the TMI accident, rather than the 360 millirems they would have received anyway. This is well below the 50,000 millirem (50 REM) exposure that holds a vanishingly slim chance of actually being harmful, and the 100 REM threshold level that holds a very tiny chance of actually producing death.

Why has TMI not become a hotbed of cancers? Because, in the words of Dr. Robert Boyar of Argonne National Laboratory, "There are no data that support a linear inference of harm from nuclear radiation down to zero effect at zero dose. The data indicate that people would live longer and healthier lives if they received a little more radiation, not less." The complete lack of negative health effects from TMI, and the lack of negative long-term health effects from Chernobyl, support Boyar's statement. The health effect data on exposures to the public from TMI and Chernobyl perfectly fit the concept of hormesis, but do not fit the no-safe-level theory.

In the thirty years since the hormesis with ionizing radiation was first discovered, numerous laboratories all over the world, from Japan to Switzerland, have come to essentially the same conclusion. In enormous doses, radiation is a deadly toxin that can, and does cause high cancer mortality. However, in low doses, such as those we experience continually as a result of living in a naturally radioactive universe, the effects provide a positive stimulation to life, and may well make life itself possible for our species. The no-safe-level theory for ionizing radiation can now be understood to be little more than a myth with respect to low level exposures!

Radiation Is an Easy "Bogey Man"

Why, then, does the no-safe-level, zero-threshold "theory" continue to be widely accepted? Dr. Boyar makes a bold statement as to the reason, "Why, in the face of the evidence, does the zero-threshold concept remain so politically correct? More to the point, consider who benefits. Are there people who make their living exploiting the zero-threshold theory? You bet! Think of the government employees at the federal, state, and local levels who use zero threshold to concoct regulations for nuclear power plants, nuclear waste disposal, radon in homes, etc. Think of the government-sponsored researchers on disposal of nuclear waste, who search for ever more esoteric ways to protect people 50,000 years hence from a conceivable, trivial addition to the natural radiation background. One might call it 'bureaucratic free enterprise.'"

Strong words, indeed. Add to this those in the public, political and environmental activist arenas whose reputations depend on their exaggerated prophecies of nuclear doom, and we can see that the business of keeping the no-safe-level myth alive is considerable. Without the public becoming aware of the truth and demanding the use of scientific correctness, this unethical practice will continue and fear of the low-level-radiation "bogey man" will endure. Once the public becomes aware of the safety concerning low level radiation exposures and makes their collective voice heard, the no-safe-level myth can be discarded and become little more than an historical point of interest similar to the false belief that the Earth is the center of the universe.

Radiation Is Invisible and Insidious . . . Right?

One of the most enduring and frightening, albeit misleading concepts concerning ionizing radiation is twofold: radiation is invisible and insidious, making it inordinately dangerous. First, radiation is invisible to the naked eye, allowing it to hide before it strikes with mortal finality. Second, radiation is insidious, lurking in sinister purpose over long periods of time before it manifests and kills us. Radiation is thus presented as the most horrific terrorist phenomena imaginable. The combined notions are misleading and used in a fashion that is unethical and morally corrupt. Each notion needs to be addressed individually in order to demonstrate their unconscionable damaging effects on the public mind.

Radiation is invisible. No doubt about it. So are all of the elements in the air we breathe. Is Oxygen or Nitrogen especially dangerous because they are invisible? Of course not. Can the air contain other invisible substances? Of course it can. Does their being invisible make them automatically deadly? Absolutely not. But, radiation is presented to the public as if it's invisible-to-the-naked-eye nature makes it singularly and uniquely dangerous because it is invisible! Of all the *hypothetically* dangerous invisible substances that might possibly surround us, radiation is probably the safest of the lot. Low levels of invisible radiation are not in the least harmful. We are exposed to radiation every moment of every day we exist. Further, our species has evolved in a naturally radioactive world, which says a lot about its safety level. Plus, it is relatively easy to detect. Radiation detectors are widespread in hospitals, research facilities, colleges, emergency centers . . . virtually everywhere. But, most people don't have one in their homes. However, Geiger counters [instruments that measure radiation] are relatively inexpensive, can be bought by anyone, and are quite easy to operate. Clearly, the invisible nature of radiation in no way makes it uniquely dangerous. In fact, low, non-lethal levels of exposure are safe and life-enhancing.

The insidious notion is even more misleading and several magnitudes more terrifying than the invisibility idea. First, most people have little or no idea what the frightening term [radiation] means. Actually, it has two overlapping meanings. One meaning is something treacherous, awaiting the best possible moment to entrap us and do us harm. Second, it is also something that has a subtle and cumulative effect on us, which builds up its lethal potential over time. The dose you receive today might not make you sick tomorrow, but if that dose continues to be received every day, over extended periods of time, it's assumed to be just as dangerous as the huge, flash doses that killed thousands at Hiroshima. In the first place, how can the most ubiquitous and constant phenomena in the universe (radiation) which has engulfed our species for the millions of years we have evolved, be singularly treacherous, hiding in silence and awaiting the optimum moment when it can suddenly inflict sinister biological havoc? It defies rational logic. Secondly, the concept that radiation exposure has a cumulative effect, building up in its terrible inevitability over time, *has no evidential foundation, whatsoever*! Yes, the notion of risk accumulation (build-up) with respect to radiation exposure has been with us since the dark days of gathering Hiroshima survivor data and the formulation of the no-safe-level hypothesis, but there is absolutely no human or laboratory animal data to support it. None! It was *assumed* as an ultra-conservative corollary to the no-safe-level hypothesis, just to err on the side of safety. Assumed, but never proven! This arbitrary assumption officially exists to this day, is one of the sovereign foundations of unnecessarily restrictive government limits on human exposures, and does little more than needlessly prolong the accumulation of avoidable psychological damage to the public from the Hiroshima Syndrome.

Radiation Has Beneficial Effects

It should be noted that current research on single living cell DNA and multi-cellular laboratory animals demonstrates the biological mechanisms at work. Low level radiation exposure actually improves an individual cell's ability to repair damage to its DNA, much the same as physical exercise improves muscle tone. It also has a cumulative effect of improved DNA repair for the remaining lifetime of the cell. In other words, radiation exposure has a positive cumulative effect in non-lethal doses, but there is no negative cumulative effect! In addition, irradiated cells tend to live longer than non-irradiated cells. These phenomena have also been found to be the case with multi-cellular laboratory animals. By increasing radiation exposure above normal background levels, living creatures experience better cellular repair functions and have longer lifetimes. There *are* accumulated health effects due to increased exposure levels, but *all* of the effects are positive, health enhancing, and life-extending.

> *"Everyone knows lots of lead or radiation or radon is bad; we'll just never know for sure whether the relationship holds at lower doses."*

The Safety Risks of Minimal Exposure to Radiation Are Unclear

Darshak Sanghavi

In the following viewpoint, Darshak Sanghavi argues that the risk factors of high-level radiation exposure are clear, because adverse effects are easily and quickly measurable, as has been shown by the Life Span Study after Hiroshima. However, Sanghavi points out, measuring the health risks of low-level radiation exposure requires the study of too many individuals over too many years. The author notes that while some researchers believe that even low-level radiation bears health risks, others assume that there is a threshold below which exposure is safe. Sanghavi is the chief of pediatric cardiology and associate professor of pediatrics at the University of Massachusetts.

Darshak Sanghavi, "Tiny Nuke—How Dangerous Are Small Doses of Radiation?," *Slate*, April 14, 2011. www.slate.com.

As you read, consider the following questions:

1. Why is it impossible to say if low-level radiation exposure poses health risks, according to the viewpoint?
2. According to the author, what are the two opposite positions regarding the risks of radiation exposure?
3. According to the author, what should replace the black-and-white dichotomy on suspected toxins?

In 1945, a profoundly sad experiment in public health began when U.S. forces dropped a 13-kiloton nuclear fission bomb on Hiroshima, Japan. Three years later, President Harry Truman ordered the National Academy of Sciences to study the long-term health effects of radiation on roughly 100,000 survivors. (A hundred thousand more perished in the blast and its immediate aftermath.) As the most rigorous research of its kind (no longitudinal study of the Chernobyl disaster's [meltdown at a nuclear power plant in the Ukraine in 1986] survivors was ever done), the Life Span Study of the Hiroshima cohort now guides almost all responses to major radiation disasters, including the recent [2011] near-meltdown at the Fukushima reactor in Japan. Yet its findings seem to have been ignored completely in the breathless reporting, over the past few weeks, of radiation contamination across the United States.

It Is Not Clear Whether We Should Worry About Low-Level Radiation

Within days of the tsunami, the nation's potassium iodide pills—which counteract the effects of radioactive iodine—sold out. The Food and Drug Administration banned vegetable and milk imports from provinces near the reactor. Just the other day, the Environmental Protection Agency reported that traces of cesium-137 had been found in milk in Vermont, while elevated levels of other radioactive isotopes were showing up in samples from Phoenix and Los Angeles. And more than a dozen cities have detected radiation in their drinking water. Despite reassurances that elevated levels of other radioactive isotopes in milk and drinking water are not dangerous, some health departments are still advising cautionary measures, like a blanket avoidance of drinking rainwater.

This contradictory advice—*don't worry! OK, worry a little . . .* arises from a fundamental scientific problem: The true health effects of low-level radiation exposure are unknowable, since any study that could identify them would require an impossibly large sample size—in the millions, not the thousands. To understand why requires a simple lesson in epidemiology.

The Case of Sadako Sasaki

While very high-dose radiation causes immediate illness and burns, the cancer-causing effects of smaller amounts don't appear for many years. Perhaps the best-known example was Sadako Sasaki, who was 2 years old when the atomic bomb code-named "Little Boy" detonated roughly one mile away from her house in Hiroshima. Sadako survived, but after turning 12, she developed unusual purple bruises on her legs and was soon diagnosed with leukemia. (As popularized in the children's book *Sadako and the Thousand Paper Cranes*, she believed she would be granted a wish if she folded 1,000 cranes but died after folding only 644.)

How do we know whether Sadako's death should be blamed on radiation exposure? The Life Span Study researchers took a very simple approach: Each victim's radiation exposure was estimated based on his or her location during the blast and compared to his or her disease outcome over the ensuing decades. Did more radiation produce more cancers? It turned out there was a pretty clear dose-response for radiation and leukemia. (The data had less to say about whether the bomb caused other kinds of cancer.) For the victims with the worst exposure—those who received a radiation dose of 4 sieverts [international system of units of radiation], or the amount you'd get from having 500 CT scans at once—there was a 20- to 40-fold increase in the risk of leukemia. At 2 sieverts, cases of leukemia were still elevated, but the risk was somewhat lower—a four-to-eightfold increase over the baseline. All told, the researchers estimated that the "Little Boy" bomb accounted for 75 additional cases of leukemia among the 100,000 survivors in the cohort, and most correlated with the highest exposure levels.

Should No Data Equal No Risk or No Threshold?

But the study had little to say about the people who received the lowest doses of radiation. Among survivors who had been exposed to something on the order of 0.15 sieverts, there was no detectable increase of risk. Does that mean that these quantities of radiation, which amount to what you'd get from two dozen CT scans, are actually harmless? Not exactly.

The perils of absorbing such doses might exist, but they could be small enough that you'd need a huge sample of victims to see them show up in the statistics. When dealing with something as uncommon as, say, leukemia (which, under normal conditions, affects less than 0.1 percent of the population over a lifetime), a small increase in risk would add just a handful of cases per decade. If you wanted to prove the risk is real, you'd need a lot of people and a very long study—far more than the 100,000 in the Hiroshima group. When it comes to measuring the effects of low doses of radiation, it's safe to say that the logistics are just too daunting, and we'll never get a satisfactory answer.

In the absence of data, the debate over low-level radiation is largely one of faith. Some researchers believe in the "linear no-threshold relationship." This mouthful assumes that if high doses of radiation impose high risks, low doses must bring their own, albeit lower, risks. On the other hand, some nuclear experts believe that low doses are harmless, and there is indeed a "threshold" below which radiation exposure can be ignored. By analogy, they might say, smoking three packs a day is bad news, but smoking one cigarette a month won't kill you.

Different Types of Radiation

Most people are familiar with sunburns. That's getting too much ultraviolet radiation exposure, whether from the sun or a tanning salon. The radiation that doctors use for X-rays and the radiation nuclear plants emit are very similar, but it's stronger than UV radiation. Sunburns stop at the skin; radiation treatment and nuclear reactor radiation go all the way through the body.

Brett, "Radiation Exposure—How Bad Is It?," Bookmark61, *March 14, 2011. http://bookmark61.xanga.com.*

Despite the lack of data on radiation exposure, most regulatory bodies conservatively adopt the no-threshold approach. That is why, for example, the Nuclear Regulatory Commission caps occupational exposure at 0.05 sieverts per year. Such fears have also driven considerable hand-wringing among doctors, who point to the four-fold increase in CT scans since the 1990s and claim that 2 percent of all cancers now are actually caused by the scans. But that's only true if there's a linear relationship between radiation exposure and cancer risk. In other words, it's assumed without any evidence that exposing a million people to 0.00001 sieverts is just as bad as exposing one person to 10 sieverts.

The Downside of the Black vs. White Approach

Is there any downside to being so conservative? Consider what happens when people think they've crossed over a "safe" limit. According to a review from the National Institutes of

Health, inchoate fears and misinformation in the wake of the Chernobyl disaster led to roughly 100,000 additional abortions among pregnant women and over 1,250 suicides. Meanwhile, outsize fears of radiation risks may lead patients and physicians to avoid necessary X-rays. Last month, the International Commission on Radiation Protection recommended that Japan temporarily raise the annual radiation limit from 0.001 sieverts to 0.02 sieverts per person, and the Tokyo Electric Power Company suddenly raised radiation worker limits to 0.15 sieverts per year. Though the changes are scientifically defensible—since no data exist showing that 0.15 sieverts are dangerous—those who believe in the no-threshold model may assume the safety of citizens and workers has been sacrificed for convenience.

Ultimately, the debate over the presence or absence of a safe threshold is the most basic divide in our society's approach to environmental regulations. Whether we argue over the safety of BPA [Bisphenol A, a solid organic compound often found in plastics] in infant bottles, lead in old houses, radiation from nuclear accidents, or trace amounts of radon in homes, we're talking about the same thing. Everyone knows lots of lead or radiation or radon is bad; we'll just never know for sure whether the relationship holds at lower doses.

Back in 1972, the nuclear physicist Alvin Weinberg presciently wrote that the dilemmas of low-dose radiation or toxic chemical exposures are "trans-scientific." To decide whether low dose radiation is dangerous would require a research project of monumental, impossible scope. Such questions, he wrote, "can be asked of science and yet cannot be answered by science. [This] elementary point has been lost in much of the public discussion of environmental hazards." The only solution was for policymakers and the public to learn to think in probabilities instead of absolutes. Instead of imposing a black-white dichotomy on suspected toxins, a graded approach—perhaps a gradient with shades of gray?—would make more sense.

Taken another way, Weinberg encouraged debates over public health regulations to acknowledge, and even embrace, uncertainty. He identified the one substance that certainly can be effective even in the smallest possible concentration: humility.

> *"Every human on Earth carries . . . a genetic footprint contaminated by the Cold War, Three Mile Island, Chernobyl, the 400-plus nuclear power plants that have not melted down and now Fukushima."*

Exposure to Radiation Is Never Safe

Brian Moench

In the following viewpoint, Brian Moench cites scientists' warnings of the dangers of nuclear radiation from the past seventy-five years. He argues that comparing the effects of nuclear radiation with the radiation emitted by a television is like comparing being hit by a table tennis ball to being hit by bullets. Moench further explains the dangers of the process of bioaccumulation, by which contaminants occur in higher concentration at the top of the food chain. Nuclear radiation, Moench concludes, causes a genetic damage that is slowly reducing our species' chance for survival. Moench is president of the Utah Physicians for a Healthy Environment.

As you read, consider the following questions:

1. What, according to the author, led President John F. Kennedy to sign the Nuclear Test Ban Treaty?
2. What does the process of bioaccumulation increase, according to the viewpoint?
3. What does Nobel Prize laureate Hermann Mueller predict, according to Moench?

Radiation from Japan is now detectable in the atmosphere, rain water and food chain in North America. Fukushima reactors [damaged by equipment failures and meltdowns following an earthquake and tsunami on March 11, 2011] are still out of control and hold 10 times more nuclear fuel than there was at Chernobyl, thousands of times more than the bomb dropped on Hiroshima. The official refrain is, "No worries here, perfectly harmless." Our best scientists of the previous century would be rolling over in their graves.

Dangerous at Any Level

In the 1940s many of the world's premier nuclear scientists saw mounting evidence that there was no safe level of exposure to nuclear radiation. This led [US physicist] Robert Oppenheimer, the father of the atom bomb, to oppose development of the hydrogen bomb.

In the 1950s, [US chemist] Linus Pauling, the only two-time winner of the Nobel Prize, began warning the public about exposure to all radiation. This opinion, ultimately endorsed by thousands of scientists worldwide, led President John F. Kennedy to sign the Nuclear Test Ban Treaty [agreement signed by the Soviet Union, the United Kingdom, and the United States on August 5, 1963, prohibiting all nuclear testing except underground tests].

In the 1960s, Drs. John Gofman, Arthur Tamplin, Alice Stewart, Thomas Mancuso and Karl Morgan, all researchers for the Atomic Energy Commission or the Department of Energy, independently came to the conclusion that exposure to nuclear radiation was not safe at any level.

The government terminated their services for coming up with what Dr. Gofman called the "wrong answer;" that is, the opposite of what the AEC wanted to hear. The top Russian nuclear physicist in the 1960s, Andrei Sakharov, also a Nobel Prize winner, and Vladimir Chernousenko, who the Soviet Union placed in charge of the Chernobyl [1986 meltdown at a nuclear power plant in the Ukraine] cleanup, are among other international experts who drew similar conclusions.

Nuclear Plants Are Not Like Televisions

To distract from the danger of man-made radioactivity, we hear from nuclear cheerleaders that watching TV and airline travel also expose us to radiation. True, although they never mention that flight crews have higher rates of breast and skin cancer. Equating those very different types of radiation is like equating the damage of being hit with ping pong balls (photons) with being hit by bullets (beta particles). Your TV doesn't shoot bullets at you.

Even if your TV only shot a few bullets per show, you probably wouldn't watch much TV. Furthermore, the damage done by these radioactive "bullets" can vary tremendously depending on which organs are hit. To carry the analogy one step further, spraying a few bullets into a large crowd can hardly be considered harmless even if the ratio of bullets per person is very low.

Bioaccumulation Is Real

Bioaccumulation increases the concentration of many contaminants as one moves up the food chain. Beef is much higher in dioxins than cattle feed and tuna fish have much higher mercury than their marine environment. Radioactive iodine, cesium, and strontium, all beta emitters, become concentrated in the food chain because of bioaccumulation. At the top of the food chain, of course, are humans, including fetuses, and human breast milk.

In 1963, one week after an atmospheric nuclear bomb test in Russia, our scientists observed the magnifying power of bioaccumulation when they detected radioactive iodine in the thyroids of mammals in North America even though they could not detect smaller amounts in the air or on vegetation.

Bioaccumulation is one reason why it is dishonest to equate the danger to humans living 5,000 miles away from Japan with the minute concentrations measured in our air. If we tried, we would now likely be able to measure radioactive iodine, cesium, and strontium bioaccumulating in human embryos in this country. Pregnant women, are you OK with that?

Radiation Endangers the Survival of Our Species

Hermann Mueller [US geneticist], another Nobel Prize winner, is one of many scientists who would not have been OK with that. In a 1964 study, "Radiation and Heredity," Mueller spelled out the genetic damage of ionizing radiation on humans. He predicted the gradual reduction of the survival of the human species as exposure to radioactivity steadily increased. Indeed, sperm counts, sperm viability and fertility rates worldwide have been dropping for decades.

These scientists and their warnings have never been disproven, but they are currently widely ignored. Their message is very clear: Virtually every human on Earth carries the nuclear legacy, a genetic footprint contaminated by the Cold War [1945–1990; the state of political hostility between the Soviet Union and its allies against the United States and its allies], Three Mile Island [Pennsylvania, nuclear power plant meltdown in 1979] Chernobyl, the 400-plus nuclear power plants that have not melted down and now Fukushima.

[German-born American physicist] Albert Einstein said, "The splitting of the atom changed everything, save man's mode of thinking; thus we drift towards unparalleled catastrophe."

> *"We have to learn lessons from Fukushima and count our blessings in the United States. And urgently start, before it is again too late."*

Spent Nuclear Fuel Pools Pose Health and National Security Risks

Najmedin Meshkati

In the following viewpoint, Najmedin Meshkati maintains that the Fukushima disaster shows that we have to prepare for improbable events. All nuclear plants in the United States dispose of nuclear waste in unsafe spent fuel pools, Meshkati explains. Their water cooling systems in the fuel pools, he asserts, are vulnerable to natural disasters and terrorist attacks. Meshkati also warns that the spent fuel pools could heat up and cause radiation contamination. Many spent fuel pools in the United States are nearing capacity, he concludes, and should slowly be decommissioned and replaced with an underground disposal site at Yucca Mountain in Nevada. Meshkati is a professor of civil/environmental, industrial, and systems engineering at the University of Southern California.

Najmedin Meshkati, "Spent Fuel Pools Are Serious Safety, Security Hazards," *Lima News*, March 22, 2011.

As you read, consider the following questions:

1. According to the author, what is the realization of probable impossibilities?
2. What potential problem could a loss of water circulation in spent fuel pools cause, according to the viewpoint?
3. What does the author state is projected to happen to the spent fuel pools in the United States over the next eleven years?

"Probable impossibilities are to be preferred to improbable possibilities." Aristotle [Greek philosopher]

An unimaginable natural disaster which was a combination of a monster 9.0 earthquake and an ensuing powerful tsunami triggered unprecedented "secondary" and "tertiary" effects of reactors meltdown, fire and radiation release at the Fukushima Daiichi Nuclear Power Station in Japan [on March 11, 2011].

A Rude Awakening

What is unfolding is the realization of probable impossibilities: The compromise of a nuclear power plant as a result of a tsunami caused by an earthquake would be a creative mind's scenario in a Hollywood disaster movie. Yet is happening before our own eyes. And it is a rude awakening to reconsider seriously our wishful assumptions of our systems' reliability and the vulnerability of the redundant safety systems to common mode failures.

Out of the six nuclear reactors at the Fukushima plant, two have had partial meltdowns, accompanied by powerful hydrogen explosions. Thankfully, their primary containment vessels, made of concrete and steel and able to prevent radiation from escaping, were mostly holding on (at least for five of the six reactors), despite the very strong motions from the earthquake. (Reactor number 2 suffered a minor breach of the primary containment.) These reactors are not out of the danger zone yet [as of March 2011] as their fuel rods contain residual heat and they need to be cooled. Most likely this will be accomplished by dumping more seawater into the vessel, then venting the resulting steam to the atmosphere and continuing this process of "feed and bleed" until they can be stabilized.

A Lethal Sauna

But at present, the gravest danger at the Fukushima plant is the dire condition of the spent fuel storage facilities which contain tons of still highly radioactive and "hot" spent fuel rods. Spent fuel (otherwise known as nuclear waste) has been of a secondary concern prior to this impending disaster, despite its immense importance. In many of nuclear plants around the world, the practice is for old rods to be stored in 30- to 40-feet deep body of water pools with a cooling system to dissipate the intense heat they give off. These pools are located in the containment area. However, loss of water or its circulation could convert the pools to a wet "lethal sauna" with rising levels of radioactive steam. An explosion last Tuesday [March 15, 2011] damaged the building of Reactor No. 4, its roof and, according to last Wednesday's [March 16, 2011] Congress testimony of the chairman of the U.S. Nuclear Regulatory Commission [NRC], resulted in all the water in these pools to boil dry. In his words: the radiation levels are extremely high, which "impact the ability to take corrective measures."

Filled to Capacity and Unsafe

Spent fuel pools are currently in use at all 65 sites with operating commercial nuclear power reactors in the United States. The unfolding nightmare in Fukushima tells us that these are major safety and security sitting ducks in 33 states of the union. A major study by the National Research Council in 2005 on the safety and security of spent fuel storage found that an accidental or a terrorist attack that "partially or completely drained the spent fuel pool could lead to a propagating zirconium cladding fire and the release of large quantities of radioactive materials to

"What'll I do with the nuclear wastes?" cartoon by Alex Faffi, www.CartoonStock.com. Copyright © Joseph Farris Reproduction rights obtainable from www.CartoonStock.com.

the environment." It recommended that "the NRC should ensure that power plant operators take prompt and effective measures to reduce the consequences of a loss-of-pool-coolant event in spent fuel pools that could result in propagating zirconium cladding fires."

More ominously, these spent fuel pools are gradually approaching their full capacity, and it is projected that up to three or four nuclear power plants will reach full capacity in their spent fuel pools, each year for at least the next eleven years [until 2022].

The Japan disaster notwithstanding, and just to highlight the urgency to paying serious attention to this issue in the United States, one can point to the dangerous safety condition of the spent fuel pool at the Unit 1 of the Millstone nuclear power plant in Connecticut, which was the subject of a protracted and controversial investigation by the NRC and was the topic of a special investigation and article in *Time* magazine. This case, according to the article, resulted in some major policy changes in the NRC, as well the inclusion of all Millstone reactors in the NRC's "hall of shame," which is the high-scrutiny "watch list" of troublesome reactors.

Lessons from Fukushima

We have to learn lessons from Fukushima and count our blessings in the United States. And urgently start, before it is again too late, decommissioning the highly risky spent fuel pools, now scattered all over the country in thirty-three states. This can be accomplished by reactivating the Yucca Mountain [Nevada] deep geologic disposal site for high-level nuclear waste, the study of which has been going on for more than twenty-five years with the staggering cost of $38 billion to date.

Making Yucca Mountain the solution to the nuclear waste disposal problem is a vital public policy issue that requires bold leadership from the administration and bipartisan support. It is fortuitous that in this critical juncture, Dr. Steven Chu, a Nobel physicist, is leading the U.S. Department of Energy. In light of what's happening in Japan, he ought to lead the effort to reconsider the decision to withdraw Yucca Mountain's license application from the NRC, restore its funding, and urgently reactivate the project.

In the age of probable impossibilities, we cannot afford to stick to wishful thinking or romantic fascination of the improbable failure of even a single one of these sixty-five dangerous sites.

Viewpoint 11

> *"[Dry] casks are designed to withstand tornados and earthquakes, and are nearly impossible to steal."*

Dry Casks Can Minimize the Health and Security Risks of Spent Nuclear Fuel Pools

Julie Wernau and Lisa Black

In the following viewpoint, Julie Wernau and Lisa Black investigate claims that dry casket storage is a safer alternative to spent fuel pools. In Zion, near Chicago, spent fuel pools will be replaced by dry cask storage by 2014, Wernau and Black explain. Experts cited in the viewpoint argue that spent fuel pools are a safety hazard due to their placement on or above ground. Dry casks, on the other hand, are designed to withstand natural disasters and terrorist attacks and, experts maintain, do not pose any danger of radiation contamination. Wernau and Black are reporters for the Chicago Tribune.

As you read, consider the following questions:

1. What is nuclear safety not designed for, according to the viewpoint?

Julie Wernau and Lisa Black, "Spent Nuclear Fuel Storage Comes Under Scrutiny," *Chicago Tribune*, March 19, 2011.

2. Why, according to the authors, are cooling pools a target for terrorists?
3. Why would even a cracked dry cask contain radiation to a small area around the cask, according to the viewpoint?

Fourteen years ago, Zion [Illinois] nuclear power plant's last red-hot fuel rod was lifted from its reactor core and submerged into a pool of water, joining the rest of the plant's 2.2 million pounds of spent fuel. The nuclear waste was supposed to be entombed deep within Nevada's Yucca Mountain.

But the U.S. Energy Department scrapped that plan last year. That left operators of Zion and more than 100 nuclear reactors in the U.S. with the responsibility for storing on site the dangerous spent fuel. Chicago-based Exelon Corp. shuttered Zion in 1998 and another company is dismantling the complex piece by piece. The plan calls for Zion's waste to be encased in concrete-and-steel bunkers not far from Lake Michigan, possibly in perpetuity.

Planning for a Once-in-a-Millennium Event

In the wake of Japan's disaster [the nuclear meltdown at the Fukushima reactor in 2011] the safety calculation involved in storing such waste has changed, experts say. More than 80 percent of the spent nuclear fuel in Illinois remains in pools.

In Japan, no one considered the possibility of a 9.0 earthquake and a devastating tsunami. Fuel rods at the crippled reactors have been exposed to air. They are heating up and emitting high levels of radiation, making it difficult for workers to get close enough to cool them. The lesson, experts say, is that nuclear safety seems more designed for most-likely scenarios, not worst-case scenarios.

"This is a once-in-a-millennium event—but we don't plan for those," Kennette Benedict, executive director and publisher of the *Bulletin of the Atomic Scientists* said Friday.

A Typical Dry Cask Storage System

At some nuclear reactors across the country, spent fuel is kept on site, above ground. . . . Once the spent fuel has cooled, it is loaded into special canisters. Each canister is designed to hold approximately 2–6 dozen spent fuel assemblies, depending on the type of assembly. Water and air are removed. The canister is filled with inert gas, and sealed (welded or bolted shut).

Some canisters are designed to be placed vertically in robust above-ground concrete or steel structures.

Some canisters are designed to be stored horizontally in above-ground concrete bunkers, each of which is about the size of a one-car garage.

United States Nuclear Regulatory Commission, "Typical Dry Cask Storage System," 2011. www.nrc.gov.

In Zion, a town of 25,000 about fifty miles north of Chicago, and at other towns where nuclear waste is stored, Japan's crisis has some questioning if the most unlikely events could happen and whether they would be protected.

In Illinois, 28,588 fuel assemblies, each containing a bundle of 200 rods and weighing about 600 pounds, are cooling in pools on the ground or above reactors as in Japan.

Positioned, up high, they are "very inviting targets for terrorists," said David Lochbaum, director of the Nuclear Safety Project of the Union of Concerned Scientists, and critics note that the buildings that house the pools are flimsy.

The Staggering Cost of Safety

"No one has come up with a solution to safely store this waste for 10,000 years into the future," said Lochbaum.

The Energy Department says it is committed to ensuring it meets its long-term disposal obligations, but a plan hasn't been disclosed.

For safety reasons, law requires spent rods to cool in pools for five years before they can be moved into dry casks—stainless-steel canisters, encased in 3-inch-thick carbon-steel liners and covered in 2 feet of reinforced concrete.

Installing dry-cask storage infrastructure at a plant with two reactors would cost between $20 million and $30 million, and annual costs for buying casks, loading them and running a dry-cask storage facility are $7 million to $10 million, according to Exelon.

Banking on Dry-Cask Storage

Unlike in Japan, Zion's fuel rods have been cooling for as long as 40 years.

"You can't have a meltdown," said Patrick Daly, general manager of EnergySolutions, which is dismantling Zion.

By 2020, EnergySolutions expects to turn the 240-acre site into an uncontaminated field of grass. Unless the federal government comes up with an alternative, 10 to 15 acres of the land will be home to 61 concrete and steel dry casks, each weighing 125 tons, used to store the spent fuel.

At a panel discussion Friday [March 18, 2011] focused on Japan's crisis and hosted by the Chicago Council on Global Affairs, Robert Gallucci, president of the John D. and Catherine T. MacArthur Foundation, said the concrete monoliths were "a good interim solution" to the storage problem. He said he was a "very enthusiastic supporter of long-term dry storage." Gallucci previously served with the U.S. State Department as a special envoy focused on the threat posed by the proliferation of weapons of mass destruction.

Even Lochbaum calls dry-cask storage "the cheapest insurance we can possibly pay."

So far, none of Zion's waste has been moved into dry casks. This summer a pad is to be built about 2,000 feet from Lake Michigan that would protect the casks from earthquakes.

Daly said spent fuel will be moved into dry casks by 2014. Meanwhile, cooling occurs through natural convection.

Nearly Impossible to Steal

The casks are designed to withstand tornados and earthquakes, and are nearly impossible to steal, Daly said. Even if a cask was cracked, hazardous levels of radiation would be contained to the area around the cask because of the age of the fuel rods, he said.

Still, some who live near Zion are concerned about permanent storage of radioactive material in the area.

Roger Whitmore, owner of a Zion automotive store and past president of the Zion Chamber of Commerce said, "If we had a big earthquake or seiche," referring to a large wave from Lake Michigan, "what's (the waste) going to do, sweep into the lake?"

That's unlikely, said Michael Chrzastowski, senior coastal geologist at the Illinois State Geological Survey. Zion is built about 9 feet above the water level of Lake Michigan. The largest seiche—a wave caused by air pressure and wind—to hit Lake Michigan was 10 feet, he said. In such a case, he said, the area would only experience "nuisance"-level flooding.

Moreover, the lake side of the storage area is protected by a wall of boulders, he said.

Of more concern, he said, is an area about 2 miles north of the Zion plant, where erosion washes away the shoreline by as much as 10 feet per year.

"Shore erosion needs to be continually monitored along the state park shore and near the power plant," he said.

Daly said they are not monitoring the erosion, but if it became a problem, the company would take care of it.

Periodical and Internet Sources Bibliography

The following articles have been chosen to supplement the diverse views presented in this chapter.

Kent Garber	"Trying to Make Nuclear Power Less Risky," *U.S. News & World Report*, March 25, 2009.
Josie Garthwaite	"How Is Japan's Nuclear Disaster Different?," *National Geographic*, March 16, 2011.
Patrick Geans-Ali	"Reminders of the Risks of Nuclear Power Come from Past/Present, Near/Far," *Huffington Post*, March 1, 2012.
Eben Harrell	"No Increased Risk of Leukemia Near Nuke Plants," *Time*, May 10, 2011.
Brian Johnson	"Nuclear Reactor Risk Assessment," *What Is Nuclear*, 2012.
Toni Johnson	"Nuclear Power Safety Concerns," Council on Foreign Relations, September 23, 2011.
Jeffrey Kluger	"Humans, Nukes and Risk Assessment: A Dangerous Mix," *Time*, March 22, 2011.
Marianne Lavell and Christina Nunez	"Pictures—Ten Oldest U.S. Nuclear Plants: Post-Japan Risks," *National Geographic*, July 19, 2011.
National Cancer Institute	"Fact Sheet: Accidents at Nuclear Power Plants and Cancer Risks," April 14, 2011.
Paul Richter and Christi Parsons	"Proposal Targets Nuclear Terrorism," *Los Angeles Times*, April 13, 2010.
Osama Tsukimori	"Japan Mayors, Governors Want Nuclear Safety Assurances," *Reuters*, March 23, 2012.
Matthew L. Wald	"Nuclear Energy: Overview," *New York Times*, October 29, 2009.

Chapter 2

Is Nuclear Power Good for the Environment?

Chapter Preface

Most of the world's energy is produced by the burning of fossil fuels such as coal, oil, and natural gas. According to the US Energy Information Administration, about 85 percent of energy in the United States is produced by the burning of fossil fuels. Because fossil fuels are not renewable, traditional ways of creating energy may not be able to meet society's ever-increasing energy needs. In addition, fossil fuels have a high carbon footprint, which means that they emit a high amount of greenhouse gases and thus contribute to global warming. Fossil fuels are a limited and damaging means of providing the world's energy supply in the future. Consequently, environmentalists urge research and support of energy sources that would replace fossil fuels. Solar, wind, and hydro power are alternatives—all renewable and with little to no lasting negative effect on the environment.

Another environmentally friendly alternative is nuclear power. Proponents of nuclear power claim that it has a low carbon footprint, mostly due to the fact that the operation of a nuclear power plant creates no carbon dioxide (CO_2) emissions. Factoring in the CO_2 emissions created when mining for raw materials as well as building and fueling the nuclear plants, the greenhouse gas emissions in the nuclear energy life-cycle are comparable to renewable forms of energy (wind and hydropower), and considerably lower than those of coal or natural gas. According to Areva, a French nuclear power conglomerate, "nuclear-generated electricity avoids almost 650 million metric tons of carbon dioxide per year in the U.S. This is nearly as much carbon dioxide as is released from all U.S. passenger cars."

Despite nuclear's low CO_2 emissions, Eben Herrell states in *Time* magazine that:

> The environmental movement has a strange historical relationship with nuclear power. In many countries, opposition to

> nuclear reactors in the wake of Chernobyl gave rise to major Green political parties. Many environmentalists still oppose nuclear power—Greenpeace, for example, still calls for the phase out of all reactors. But as climate change has taken over the Green agenda, other environmentalists have come to favor nuclear as part of a low-carbon energy mix. It was this confluence of factors—fading memories of Chernobyl and increased concern about greenhouse gases—that gave the nuclear industry such confidence just a few years ago. That confidence will have been deeply shaken by events in Japan.

The Fukushima disaster does not paint an environmentally friendly picture: Radioactivity escaped into the air and the ground water, the area around the plants will be uninhabitable for decades, and one year after the event, decommissioning the damaged plants proves more difficult than expected. The Associated Press reports: "The data shows the damage from the disaster is so severe the plant operator will have to develop special equipment and technology to tolerate the harsh environment, and decommission the plant. The process is expected to last decades."

Even putting accidents such as Fukushima aside, environmentalists argue that a "transition from coal to an equally dangerous source—nuclear power . . . is not a climate solution." GreenAmerica.org holds that nuclear power "may produce lower-carbon energy, but it is not clean energy," and goes on to state that:

> The waste from nuclear power plants will be toxic for humans for more than 100,000 years. . . . Nuclear proponents hope that the next generation of nuclear plants will generate much less waste, but this technology is not yet fully developed or proven. Even if new technology eventually can successfully reduce the waste involved, the waste that remains will still be toxic for 100,000 years."

The authors of the viewpoints in this chapter discuss whether nuclear power is a clean environmentally friendly and sustainable energy source, if its low carbon emissions outweigh the environmental hazards of nuclear waste, and if environmental concerns can be addressed by improved nuclear technology.

VIEWPOINT 1

> *"Atomic energy has just been subjected to one of the harshest of possible tests, and the impact on people and the planet has been small."*

Nuclear Energy Is Still a Safe Alternative Energy Source and Should Be Developed

George Monbiot

In the following viewpoint George Monbiot explains how the 2011 disaster that destroyed the Fukushima Power Plant has made him a supporter of nuclear power. Even though the Fukushima reactor was poorly designed, badly maintained, and hit by a major tsunami, Monbiot maintains, no one has died as a result of radiation, which proves that nuclear power is relatively safe. Monbiot asserts that environmental advocates have overstated the dangers of nuclear power and minimized the harmful effects of other forms of renewable energy. Nuclear power, Monbiot declares, has a much smaller impact on the environment than many other forms of renewable energy and is also more efficient. Monbiot is a columnist for the Guardian *and an environmental activist.*

George Monbiot, "Why Fukushima Made Me Stop Worrying and Love Nuclear Power," *The Guardian*, March 21, 2011.

As you read, consider the following questions:

1. What does the author claim has been widely exaggerated by the "greens"?
2. According to the author, how should renewable energy be used?
3. Which energy source does the author believe most economies will revert to if they abandon nuclear power?

You will not be surprised to hear that the events in Japan [the meltdown at the Fukushima nuclear power plant in 2011] have changed my view of nuclear power. You will be surprised to hear how they have changed it. As a result of the disaster at Fukushima, I am no longer nuclear-neutral. I now support the technology.

The Dangers of Radiation Have Been Exaggerated

A crappy old plant with inadequate safety features was hit by a monster earthquake and a vast tsunami. The electricity supply failed, knocking out the cooling system. The reactors began to explode and melt down. The disaster exposed a familiar legacy of poor design and corner-cutting. Yet, as far as we know, no one has yet received a lethal dose of radiation.

Some greens [those advocating environmentally friendly practices] have-wildly exaggerated the dangers of radioactive pollution. . . . [A] graphic published by xkcd.com . . . shows that the average total dose from the Three Mile Island disaster [the 1979 meltdown at a nuclear power plant in Pennsylvania] for someone living within 10 miles of the plant was one 625th of the maximum yearly amount permitted for US radiation workers. This, in turn, is half of the lowest one-year dose clearly linked to an increased cancer risk, which, in its turn, is one 80th of an invariably fatal exposure. I'm not proposing complacency here. I am proposing perspective.

If other forms of energy production caused no damage, these impacts would weigh more heavily. But energy is like medicine: if there are no side-effects, the chances are that it doesn't work.

Renewable Energy Sources Also Have Drawbacks

Like most greens, I favour a major expansion of renewables. I can also sympathise with the complaints of their opponents. It's not just the onshore windfarms that bother people, but also the new grid connections (pylons and power lines). As the proportion of renewable electricity on the grid rises, more pumped storage will be needed to keep the lights on. That means reservoirs on mountains: they aren't popular, either.

The impacts and costs of renewables rise with the proportion of power they supply, as the need for storage and redundancy increases. It may well be the case (I have yet to see a comparative study) that up to a certain grid penetration—50% or 70%, perhaps—renewables have smaller carbon impacts than nuclear, while beyond that point, nuclear has smaller impacts than renewables.

Like others, I have called for renewable power to be used both to replace the electricity produced by fossil fuel and to expand the total supply, displacing the oil used for transport and the gas used for heating fuel. Are we also to demand that it replaces current nuclear capacity? The more work we expect renewables to do, the greater the impact on the landscape will be, and the tougher the task of public persuasion.

But expanding the grid to connect people and industry to rich, distant sources of ambient energy [harvested from natural or human-made sources] is also rejected by most of the greens who complained about the blog post I wrote last week [March 2011] in which I argued that nuclear remains safer than coal. What they want, they tell me, is something quite different: we should power down and produce our energy locally. Some have even called for the abandonment of the grid. Their bucolic vision sounds lovely, until you read the small print.

At high latitudes like ours, most small-scale ambient power production is a dead loss. Generating solar power in the UK involves a spectacular waste of scarce resources. It's hopelessly inefficient and poorly matched to the pattern of demand. Wind power in populated areas is largely worthless. This is partly because we have built our settlements in sheltered places; partly because turbulence caused by the buildings interferes with the airflow and chews up the mechanism. Micro-hydropower might work for a farmhouse in Wales, but it's not much use in Birmingham.

And how do we drive our textile mills, brick kilns, blast furnaces and electric railways—not to mention advanced industrial processes? Rooftop solar panels? The moment you consider the demands of the whole economy is the moment at which you fall out of love with local energy production. A national (or, better still, international) grid is the essential prerequisite for a largely renewable energy supply.

We Cannot Turn Back the Energy Clock

Some greens go even further: why waste renewable resources by turning them into electricity? Why not use them to provide energy directly? To answer this question, look at what happened in Britain before the industrial revolution.

The damming and weiring of British rivers for watermills was small-scale, renewable, picturesque and devastating. By blocking the rivers and silting up the spawning beds, they helped bring to an end the gigantic runs of migratory fish that were once among our great natural spectacles and which fed much of Britain—wiping out sturgeon, lampreys and shad, as well as most sea trout and salmon.

Traction [hauling of goods and raw materials along tracks] was intimately linked with starvation. The more land that was set aside for feeding draft animals for industry and transport, the less was available for feeding humans. It was the 17th-century equivalent of today's biofuels crisis. The same applied to heating fuel. As EA Wrigley points out in his book *Energy and the English Industrial Revolution*, the 11m tonnes of coal mined in England in 1800 produced as much energy as 11m acres of woodland (one third of the land surface) would have generated.

Before coal became widely available, wood was used not just for heating homes but also for industrial processes: if half the land surface of Britain had been covered with woodland, Wrigley shows, we could have made 1.25m tonnes of bar iron a year (a fraction of current consumption) and nothing else. Even with a much lower population than today's, manufactured goods in the land-based economy were the preserve of the elite. Deep green energy production—decentralised, based on the products of the land—is far more damaging to humanity than nuclear meltdown.

There Are No Harmless Alternative Fuel Sources

But the energy source to which most economies will revert if they shut down their nuclear plants is not wood, water, wind or sun, but fossil fuel. On every measure (climate change, mining impact, local pollution, industrial injury and death, even radioactive discharges) coal is 100 times worse than nuclear power. Thanks to the expansion of shale gas production, the impacts of natural gas are catching up fast.

Yes, I still loathe the liars who run the nuclear industry. Yes, I would prefer to see the entire sector shut down, if there were harmless alternatives. But there are no ideal solutions. Every energy technology carries a cost; so does the absence of energy technologies. Atomic energy has just been subjected to one of the harshest of possible tests, and the impact on people and the planet has been small. The crisis at Fukushima has converted me to the cause of nuclear power.

"Nuclear power will never live up to industry promises. As a whole it is ultimately unsafe, an accident waiting to happen, and far more expensive than proponents admit."

Nuclear Power Poses Threats to Safety and the Environment and Should Be Scrapped

Paul Josephson

In the following viewpoint Paul Josephson cites seven reasons why nuclear power is not a viable and economic power source. Most nuclear reactors are near major population centers, Josephson asserts, and evacuation in case of an emergency is difficult. To increase economic feasibility, the life span of nuclear reactors has been increased to forty years, he notes, and older reactors do not comply with safety standards. Josephson also warns that nuclear waste cannot be stored safely, nuclear plants are vulnerable to terrorism, natural catastrophes cannot be predicted, and nuclear energy is not cost effective. Renewable energies are safer and cheaper, he concludes. Josephson is chair of the history department at Colby College in Waterville, Maine.

Paul Josephson, "Japan Nuclear Crisis: Seven Reasons Why We Should Abandon Nuclear Power," *Christian Science Monitor*, March 14, 2011.

As you read, consider the following questions:

1. According to the author, what has Hurricane Katrina shown?
2. What would be particularly difficult with "floating" nuclear power stations, according to the viewpoint?
3. According to the author, what is not included in reactor costs?

The disaster at the Fukushima Daiichi nuclear power station in Japan [in 2011] underscores—yet again—the need to abandon nuclear power as a panacea for energy independence. Experts may never determine what caused all of the emergency cooling safety systems at Daiichi to fail completely. But they have learned that they are nearly powerless to bring the smoldering units under control. In the meantime, significant amounts of radioactive gas have vented, and partial meltdowns of at least two reactors have occurred. Indeed, nuclear power will never live up to industry promises. As a whole it is ultimately unsafe, an accident waiting to happen, and far more expensive than proponents admit.

Colby College professor Paul Josephson gives seven reasons why we should abandon nuclear power and instead turn to solar, wind, and other forms of energy production that won't experience such catastrophic accidents.

Nuclear Accidents and Population Centers

Worldwide standard operating procedures at nuclear power plants offer little margin for safety errors, and the industry is scrambling to check safety at each station. But can it reliably prevent another accident? Accidents are difficult to predict and have immediate far-reaching consequences, compounded by the fact that most nuclear reactors are located near major population centers—Moscow, Boston, Chicago, Los Angeles, Budapest, Kiev. It is nearly impossible to evacuate hundreds of thousands of people in a timely fashion, even with advance warning of several days—as hurricane Katrina demonstrated in New Orleans.

Officials at the Japanese nuclear plant did not think to have closed-circuit cameras inside the buildings to chart an accident for which they never fully planned. But we can be certain of the following: Officials belatedly warned surrounding residents of the danger to their lives, belatedly began to issue potassium iodide tablets to protect them, and belatedly expanded the evacuation zone around the station. Now at least 100,000 people have had to leave the area, and at least 100,000 more have been forced to live inside of sealed houses. At Chernobyl [site of a nuclear meltdown on April 26, 1986], as well, the authorities only ordered evacuation after a shocking delay.

Old Reactors Are Dangerous

It is now standard practice to extend the life of reactors from their design parameters of 25 years to 40 years and longer. It seems foolish at best to take such a gamble on complex technology that operates under high temperature and pressure. Any "unlikely" loss of coolant-capacities may result in explosions, meltdown, and significant release of radioactivity into the environment.

No Secure Repository for Spent Fuel Exists

Utilities and reactor operators still store spent fuel and other nuclear waste in and around reactors, since no truly secure, permanent repository has been built. In the US, 70,000 tons of spent fuel sits at 103 reactors around the country within 75 miles of 125 million people. In Russia, 50,000 tons of spent fuel remains at power stations.

Reactors Are Vulnerable to Terrorism

Reactors around the world—55 in Japan, 103 in the US, 40 in Russia, and so on—are also vulnerable to terrorism. For example, a National Academy of Sciences report in 2005 indicated that

Japanese Nobel Laureate Kenzaburo Oe Urges Japan to Abandon Nuclear Power

One hopes that the accident at the Fukushima facility will allow the Japanese . . . to recognize the danger of nuclear power, and to put an end to the illusion of the efficacy of deterrence that is advocated by nuclear powers.

Kenzaburo Oe, "Tokyo Postcard: History Repeats," New Yorker, *March 28, 2011.*

pools holding spent fuel stored at these reactors might not withstand a determined attack. The industry is now touting—and building—"floating" nuclear power stations that would operate on barges; clearly protection of these stations would be difficult.

Mother Nature's Threat

As the nuclear crisis in Japan has shown, even the best-prepared facilities can neither predict nor withstand the most severe natural disasters. Exacerbating the inherent dangers of nuclear power, several plants have been built on active seismic faults: Diablo Canyon in California, Metsamor in Armenia, and Fukushima in Japan.

Diablo Canyon in California is designed to withstand a 7.5 magnitude quake, but experts have raised serious concerns—even before Japan's 8.9-magnitude earthquake and tsunami—that the plant's safety would be threatened by a tsunami or high-magnitude earthquake.

The Metsamor Nuclear Power Plant in Armenia had to close abruptly in 1988 because of a devastating earthquake. It was restarted seven years later to cope with the country's energy shortage, but has since been condemned by the European Union as deeply unsafe and vulnerable to accident.

The Costs of Nuclear Energy Outweigh Its Benefits

For fifty years, engineers have promised "too cheap to meter" energy, the construction of inherently safe reactors, and solution to waste disposal. Instead, a typical reactor, based on the experience of the advanced French industry, now costs a minimum of $6 billion. The Obama administration approved $54 billion in subsidies to the nuclear industry to jumpstart construction in the US.

Reactor costs do not include transmission, waste disposal, fuel costs, or the great costs of remediating such accidents as Three Mile Island [a 1979 meltdown at a nuclar power plant in Pennsylvania], Chernobyl, and now Fukushima Daiichi. These billions of dollars will buy only more risk to the general population.

Renewable Energies Are Safer and Cheaper

With each accident—Three Mile Island, Chernobyl, Fukushima Daiichi—the nuclear industry has followed the same pattern: hesitation to inform the public about the dangers as matters go from bad to worse, followed by assertions that none of the world's other reactors can face the same fate.

Yet none of these risks and dangers exist with other, renewable forms of energy—wind energy, solar energy—and conservation. If they are costly now in terms of power generation, they end up being less expensive and safer, while Fukushima Daiichi has already entered the lexicon of terrifying nuclear accidents.

Viewpoint 3

> *"Reprocessing would make it easier for terrorists to acquire nuclear weapons materials, and for nations to develop nuclear weapons programs."*

Nuclear Reprocessing Is an Environmental Hazard and Creates Obstacles to Effective Waste Management

Union of Concerned Scientists

In the following viewpoint, the Union of Concerned Scientists argues that reprocessing nuclear waste increases the risk of nuclear terrorism because reprocessed plutonium is no longer stored in huge, highly radioactive pools, and is thus easier to steal. Reprocessing technologies, the group notes, can be misappropriated for making nuclear weapons. The group maintains that focusing on reprocessing plutonium is too expensive, ineffective, and distracts from attempts to improve geological disposal. Finally, the Union of Concerned Scientists concludes, reprocessing plutonium does not decrease the need for storage and disposal of nuclear waste, because plutonium only constitutes a small percentage of nuclear waste. The Union of Concerned Scientists is a non-profit organization that advocates for a healthy and safe environment.

Union of Concerned Scientists, "Nuclear Reprocessing: Dangerous, Dirty, and Expensive," April 5, 2011. www.ucsusa.org.

As you read, consider the following questions:

1. How much plutonium is needed to make a nuclear weapon, according to the viewpoint?
2. According to the author, why can the United States not persuade other countries to forego using fuel cycle technologies?
3. In the author's opinion, how does reprocessing make nuclear waste management more difficult?

Reprocessing is a series of chemical operations that separates plutonium and uranium from other nuclear waste contained in the used (or "spent") fuel from nuclear power reactors. The separated plutonium can be used to fuel reactors, but also to make nuclear weapons. In the late 1970s, the United States decided on nuclear non-proliferation grounds not to reprocess spent fuel from U.S. power reactors, but instead to directly dispose of it in a deep underground geologic repository where it would remain isolated from the environment for at least tens of thousands of years.

While some supporters of a U.S. reprocessing program believe it would help solve the nuclear waste problem, reprocessing would not reduce the need for storage and disposal of radioactive waste. Worse, reprocessing would make it easier for terrorists to acquire nuclear weapons materials, and for nations to develop nuclear weapons programs.

Reprocessing Would Increase the Risk of Nuclear Terrorism

Less than twenty pounds of plutonium is needed to make a simple nuclear weapon. If the plutonium remains bound in large, heavy, and highly radioactive spent fuel assemblies (the current U.S. practice), it is nearly impossible to steal. In contrast, separated plutonium is not highly radioactive and is stored in a concentrated powder form. Some claim that new reprocessing technologies that would leave the plutonium blended with other elements, such as neptunium, would result in a mixture that would be too radioactive to steal. This is incorrect; neither neptunium nor the other elements under consideration are radioactive enough to preclude theft. Most of these other elements are also weapon-usable.

Moreover, commercial-scale reprocessing facilities handle so much of this material that it has proven impossible to keep track of it accurately in a timely manner, making it feasible that the theft of enough plutonium to build several bombs could go undetected for years.

A U.S. reprocessing program would add to the worldwide stockpile of separated and vulnerable civil plutonium that sits in storage today, which totaled roughly 250 metric tons as of the end of 2009—enough for some 30,000 nuclear weapons. Reprocessing the U.S. spent fuel generated to date would increase this by more than 500 metric tons.

Reprocessing Would Increase the Ease of Nuclear Proliferation

U.S. reprocessing would undermine the U.S. goal of halting the spread of fuel cycle technologies that are permitted under the Nuclear Non-Proliferation Treaty but can be used to make nuclear weapons materials. The United States cannot credibly persuade other countries to forgo a technology it has newly embraced for its own use. Although some reprocessing advocates claim that new reprocessing technologies under development will be "proliferation resistant," they would actually be more difficult for international inspectors to safeguard because it would be harder to make precise measurements of the weapon-usable materials during and after processing. Moreover, all reprocessing technologies are far more proliferation-prone than direct disposal.

Reprocessing Would Hurt U.S. Nuclear Waste Management Efforts

First, there is no spent fuel storage crisis that warrants such a drastic change in course. Hardened interim storage of spent fuel

"Someone's put nuclear waste in the paper bin again!"

"Someone's put nuclear waste in the paper bin again!" cartoon by Bill Proud. www.CartoonStock.com. Copyright © BART. Reproduction rights obtainable from www.CartoonStock.com

in dry casks is an economically viable and secure option for at least fifty years.

Second, reprocessing does not reduce the need for storage and disposal of radioactive waste, and a geologic repository would still be required. Plutonium constitutes only about one percent of the spent fuel from U.S. reactors. After reprocessing, the remaining material will be in several different waste forms, and the total volume of nuclear waste will have been increased by a factor of twenty or more, including low-level waste and plutonium-contaminated waste. The largest component of the remaining material is uranium, which is also a waste product because it is contaminated and undesirable for reuse in reactors. Even if the uranium is classified as low-level waste, new low-level nuclear waste facilities would have to be built to dispose of it. And to make a significant reduction in the amount of high-level nuclear waste that would require disposal, the used fuel would need to be reprocessed and reused many times with an extremely high degree of efficiency—an extremely difficult endeavor that would likely take centuries to accomplish.

Finally, reprocessing would divert focus and resources from a U.S. geologic disposal program and hurt—not help—the U.S. nuclear waste management effort. The licensing requirements for the reprocessing, fuel fabrication, and waste processing plants would dwarf those needed to license a repository, and provide additional targets for public opposition. What is most needed today is a renewed focus on secure interim storage of spent fuel and on gaining the scientific and technical consensus needed to site a geological repository.

Reprocessing Would Be Very Expensive

Reprocessing and the use of plutonium as reactor fuel are also far more expensive than using uranium fuel and disposing of the spent fuel directly. In the United States, some 60,000 tons of nuclear waste have already been produced, and existing reactors add some 2,000 metric tons of spent fuel annually. The Energy Department recently released an industry estimate that a reprocessing plant with an annual capacity of 2,000 metric tons of spent fuel would cost up to $20 billion to build—and the U.S. would need two of these to reprocess all its spent fuel. An

Argonne National Laboratory scientist recently estimated that the cost premium for reprocessing spent fuel would range from 0.4 to 0.6 cents per kilowatt-hour—corresponding to an extra $3 to $4.5 billion per year for the current U.S. nuclear reactor fleet. The American public would end up having to pay this charge, either through increased taxes or higher electricity bills.

VIEWPOINT 4

"The growing need for low-carbon nuclear energy has led to a reassessment of the nation's long-term used fuel management program."

Advanced Technologies Can Make Nuclear Reprocessing Safe and Efficient

Nuclear Energy Institute

In the following viewpoint, the Nuclear Energy Institute (NEI) supports a three-fold approach to used nuclear fuel disposal that incorporates interim storage, research into reprocessing technologies, and permanent storage. Citing the growing need for low-carbon nuclear energy, the institute argues that the US government should research technologies for advanced reprocessing and recycling. Efficient nuclear reprocessing will take decades to develop and some nuclear waste will always remain, the institute acknowledges, but maintains that the usage and research of several newer technologies in other countries such as France and Great

"Advanced Fuel-Cycle Technologies Hold Promise for Used Fuel Management Program," *Policy Brief of the Nuclear Energy Institute*, March 2010. www.nei.org.

Britain is promising. The NEI is the policy organization of the nuclear industry.

As you read, consider the following questions:

1. What drives the development of advanced fuel-cycle technologies, according to the author?
2. According to the viewpoint how long does reactor and/or geologic disposal fuel remain in the reactor before it is disposed of as waste?
3. What does the process called PUREX do, according to the viewpoint?

- The growing need for low-carbon nuclear energy has led to a reassessment of the nation's long-term used fuel management program, including interest in advanced reprocessing and recycling of used nuclear fuel, advanced fuel fabrication, and development of new reactor designs that could further minimize byproducts of the uranium fuel cycle.
- The federal government and industry should pursue research into advanced recycling and reactor technologies as well as development of existing technologies. However, no advanced technology will preclude the need for a federal geologic repository for the ultimate byproducts of recycling used nuclear fuel.
- In the interim period, storage of used reactor and/or geologic disposal fuel at willing host locations would enable safe and secure management of the used fuel until recycling facilities are available.
- The expected growth of nuclear energy in the United States and around the world is a key driver behind development of advanced fuel-cycle technologies. Any decision to pursue advanced fuel cycles must consider the economic and nonproliferation factors associated with recycling uranium fuel.

The Nuclear Energy Industry Supports Integrated Used Fuel Management Strategy

The nuclear energy industry supports a three-pronged, integrated used fuel management strategy that includes:

- centralized interim storage
- research, development, commercial demonstration and deployment at the right time of technologies to reprocess and recycle uranium fuel
- development of a permanent geologic disposal facility

Used fuel storage at nuclear plant sites is safe and secure. However, consolidated storage sites at willing host locations would enable the movement of used fuel from both operating and decommissioned nuclear plants before recycling and/or geologic disposal facilities begin operating.

The industry supports the development of advanced nuclear fuel cycles, which will take decades to complete. The pursuit of this longer-term objective needs to begin in the near term; however, these activities must not compromise the federal government's obligation under the Nuclear Waste Policy Act to manage used commercial reactor fuel.

Evaluating Closing the Fuel Cycle for the Long Term

The United States, for economic and other reasons, does not recycle used nuclear fuel. Commercial reactor fuel remains in the reactor for three or four years. Under current U.S. policy, that fuel then is to be removed for disposal in a specially designed repository. However, other nations such as France, Japan and the United Kingdom (until early 2012) use a fuel cycle in which used reactor fuel is reprocessed and recycled into new fuel for reactors. Ultimately, the remaining byproducts will be sent to a repository for disposal.

99 Percent of Nuclear Energy Is Wasted

Reprocessing is the chemical separation of energy-usable materials from used nuclear fuel. It permits full use of nuclear materials that would provide a virtually inexhaustible energy resource that does not add pollutants to the atmosphere. It is also needed to separate weapons-usable materials from nuclear wastes so that the weapons-usable materials can be transmuted [converted] to non-weapons materials for beneficial use, and the wastes disposed of without need for indefinite safeguards, which cannot be assured.

Nuclear power plants in the United States and most nations use less than 1 percent of the energy in nuclear materials. In the best possible reprocessing concept, essentially *all* of the products produced in nuclear reactors could be recovered and put to beneficial uses.

Decision-makers for every light water reactor built in the world to date had the full expectation that spent fuel would be reprocessed, the remaining energy values would be recycled for production of energy, and the weapons-usable plutonium would be destroyed in producing pollution-free electricity.

Reprocessing, integrated with mixed uranium-plutonium fuel fabrication in a well-designed, well-managed fuel recycle complex, would assure that weapons-usable materials would remain inaccessible until they were transmuted to non-weapons usable materials. Reprocessing and recycle are thus essential components of good nonproliferation practice.

Clinton Bastin, "We Need to Reprocess Spent Nuclear Fuel and Can Do It Safely, at Reasonable Cost." 21st Century Science and Technology, *Summer 2008, pp. 10–11.*

Recycling of used fuel has the potential to reduce the need for new uranium supply and enrichment services. It also has the potential to provide greater utilization of a geological repository and lower the risk to the biosphere from the high-level radioactive material stored there.

In the United States, reprocessing and recycling would entail the following:

- establishing the policy and regulatory requirements for recycling facilities
- developing advanced used fuel recycling techniques
- deploying new fuel designs in existing reactors
- developing advanced reactors to extract additional energy from the recycled fuel and further reduce the volume, heat and radiotoxicity of byproducts in the fuel
- developing a federal repository

Development of these new technologies will take time. It is appropriate that the federal government begin to vigorously pursue development of these technologies.

Advanced fuel-cycle technologies cannot eliminate all of the byproducts in used nuclear fuel. Moreover, the systems eventually developed may not have the capacity to recycle all the commercial used fuel ever generated. The United States still will need a federal repository for disposal of these byproducts and for any unreprocessed used nuclear fuel. Repository disposal also is needed for the high-level radioactive waste created by the federal government from its defense programs. Most of this material is stored temporarily in Idaho, South Carolina and Washington.

Advanced fuel cycle technologies would capture some of the unused energy remaining in uranium fuel after a single "once-through" cycle in a reactor and could reduce the volume, heat and toxicity of radioactive byproducts for repository disposal.

Looking to the Future

Today's reprocessing technology—known as PUREX—makes it possible to recycle and reuse the uranium and plutonium from used nuclear fuel. The remaining waste products are mainly unusable fission products, which are mixed with glass for disposal as high-level radioactive waste in a process known as vitrification.

The uranium and plutonium separated from used reactor fuel by PUREX reprocessing can be recycled as mixed oxide fuel. This process has been used in a safe and proliferation-resistant manner. The PUREX process produces plutonium that is stored under strict security and safeguards as provided in internationally agreed protocols. Japan is building a reprocessing facility that uses a modified PUREX process that mixes uranium with the plutonium product. The new facility is scheduled to start operating by the end of 2010 [latest date unknown].

Advanced reprocessing systems do not separate plutonium; rather, they keep uranium, plutonium and other usable elements together, while separating radioactive byproducts that have no energy value. One such process, called UREX+, extracts the fission products from used fuel, leaving the remaining plutonium mixed with uranium and other elements. These uranium isotopes are extracted with the plutonium and recycled as fuel for advanced reactors. UREX+ produces high-level radioactive waste requiring disposal. Although proven in laboratories, UREX+ is not yet commercially proven.

The French are developing a process called COEX, which extracts uranium and plutonium together. In the United States, the Department of Energy also is developing other processes, such as "pyroprocessing," [method of processing involving high heat] that use metallurgical technology. The private sector is proposing other processes to accomplish the same goal.

Finally, a new generation of liquid metal-cooled and fast reactor technologies could provide nuclear fuel cycle services, such as breeding new fuel and consuming recycled nuclear waste as fuel. They could support government-sponsored nonproliferation efforts by consuming material from former nuclear weapons, thus eliminating them as a threat.

The industry believes that to realize fully the long-term benefits of nuclear energy, the United States and other nations must develop advanced fuel-cycle technologies that will supply recycled fuel when it is appropriate to do so, while reducing the amount of radioactive byproducts requiring disposal in a specially designed repository.

"Nuclear power is projected as being the lowest cost means of generating electrical energy, and by far the cheapest way to displace carbon from energy production."

Nuclear Power Can Help Fight Global Warming

Colin McInnes

In the following viewpoint, professor Colin McInnes traces the history of energy production from wood to coal to oil to nuclear energy, arguing that the increasing energy density and efficiency of these sources has de-carbonized energy production. Renewable energy sources require a massive and costly infrastructure to deliver reliable energy, McInnes contends, while nuclear power is the most efficient and sustainable low-carbon energy source available. Because uranium is virtually limitless given the fact that spent fuel can be reprocessed, he concludes, nuclear power is the technology of a low-carbon future. McInnes is professor of engineering science at the University of Strathclyde in Scotland.

Colin McInnes, "Nuclear Energy—The Key to a Low-Carbon Future," *Caledonian Mercury*, February 2, 2011. http://biztech.caledonianmercury.com.

As you read, consider the following questions:

1. How does energy density affect energy efficiency, according to the viewpoint?
2. According to the author, what negative effects does wind power have on the environment?
3. According to the author, is uranium a finite energy source?

Scotland has ambitious plans to become a world leading low carbon economy. But to deliver on this ambition will take some clear thinking about how we will generate energy in the future. More importantly, we need to learn from our past and recognise that we have been decarbonising our economy for nearly 400 years.

The beginning of the substitution of coal for wood during the Elizabethan era was our first transition to a low carbon economy. Surprisingly, coal is a low carbon fuel since per unit of energy produced it releases less carbon than wood. As noted by Jesse Ausubel at The Rockefeller University, this decarbonising of energy production has continued through waves of energy transitions from coal to oil, methane and now nuclear fission. Each new fuel has a higher energy density and a lower carbon content than the last, particularly so for carbon-free nuclear energy. For example, one kilogram of coal can power a light bulb for 4 days, one kilogram of methane for 6 days and one kilogram of uranium for a remarkable 140 years.

Slow Substitution of High Carbon with Low Carbon Energy Sources

These continuous improvements in energy density have led to better energy utility, falling energy costs and wonderfully, greater energy use. Of course our growing energy use has led to an overall increase in carbon emissions. But let's not forget, this growth in emissions correlates strongly with the extraordinary improvements in human well-being since the industrial revolution.

In the Elizabethan era, coal was seen as a dirty and polluting fuel. Some thinkers such as agricultural writer Arthur Standish advocated simply growing more trees to meet rising energy demand and so avoid the use of coal at all costs. Writing in 1615 Standish claims "there may be as much timber raised as will maintain the kingdom for all uses forever". Such a national energy policy would no doubt have led to a sustainable society based on renewable biomass, but it would never have led to the marvels of the industrial revolution and the liberating and civilising effects of cheap energy. Later, with the advent of coal-driven steam power through the innovations of [Scottish inventor] James Watt, energy costs fell while prosperity rose for the first time in human history. Carbohydrate fuelled human labour was replaced with hydrocarbon fuelled machines. This is human progress.

Wood is a diffuse energy source and required much human labour to gather and use. As practical wood resource limits were reached in the neighbourhood of population centres, transportable, energy dense coal slowly became the fuel of choice for warmth and emerging industries. Such was the shortage of wood in central Scotland during the reign of James VI it was quipped that, "if Judas had repented in the king's native land [Scotland], he would have been hard put to find a tree on which to hang himself". The growing use of coal helped end the Elizabethan energy crisis (which peaked between 1570 and 1630) and allowed an escape from the Malthusian trap of medieval subsistence.

The transition from low energy, carbon rich wood from forests to low carbon, energy rich coal from the ground which began in the 17th century was our first step in de-coupling energy production from the environment. Due to its poor energy density wood required vast areas of forest to be levelled for energy production, demonstrating the strong coupling between the environment and energy production from diffuse sources. In comparison, energy dense coal could be extracted from compact punctiform mines, while oil from the ground would start to replace oil from whales later at the end of the 19th century.

This important coupling between energy density and environmental impact can be seen again in the steady growth of wind farms across Scotland to exploit diffuse renewable energy. Current plans are for the 5 TW-hr of energy produced by onshore wind in 2008 to grow to almost 20 TW-hr by 2030. At the same time the 14.3 TW-hr of nuclear energy produced by Huntertson B and Torness in 2008 will vanish by 2030. The sole result of this energy transition is that we will have substituted 15 TW-hr per year of compact, base-load nuclear energy for the same quantity of diffuse, intermittent wind energy. In the process we will have expanded onshore wind farms fourfold and disfigured many unique Scottish landscapes.

The long history of energy production in Scotland, from Elizabethan-era woodland to Victorian lowland coal, North Sea oil and gas and now nuclear fission shows a slow substitution of fuels, with energy transitions coming in waves. In terms of its long-term historical market share, coal is in its twilight years while methane and uranium are in the ascendancy. The beginning of the large-scale use of civil nuclear energy in Scotland since the opening of the 1200 MW Hunterston B plant in 1976 (currently operating at 870 MW) is simply the most recent wave in a 400 year journey along a path of improving energy density and falling carbon intensity.

Renewable Energies Require a Massive Infrastructure

In a strong parallel to the Elizabethan aversion to coal, some now advocate avoiding the use of uranium at all costs by returning entirely to the large-scale use of diffuse and intermittent energy sources such as wind. While the wind, waves and sun are of course free, the massive infrastructure to gather low grade, diffuse renewable energy, turn it into to high grade, concentrated electrical energy and deliver it along lengthy transmission systems to urban population centres is not. Renewable energy such as wind requires immense quantities of materials—principally steel and concrete. In comparison, per unit of energy produced, compact nuclear plants are vastly more efficient in their use of materials due to the energy density of their fuel and their long design life of 60 years compared to 20 years for renewables.

Support for renewable energy is provided through renewable obligation certificates. The key word is obligation. There is a legislated requirement to continually grow renewable energy production to meet entirely arbitrary European targets. Renewable energy is growing, not because it is a more productive means of generating energy, but because government has mandated it and is providing extremely generous incentives.

For example, the 322 MW Whitelees wind farm at Eaglesham generated 676,133 MW-hr of fluctuating electrical energy last year, supported by renewables obligation certificates worth £37.5 per MW-hr. This amounts to £24M of revenue, or some £480M over the 20 year life of the wind farm, paid for through higher energy bills. This is a seriously good return on a £300M capital investment, and that's before revenue from the sale of electricity. It should be no surprise that developers have been queuing up for a slice of Scotland. Ambitious plans for 11,000 MW of offshore wind will require some £30B of capital and potentially up to £57B of renewable obligation costs over the 20 year life of offshore plant. This will be exceptionally expensive energy. It is not clear who will buy such energy in an export market, or what will be the result of a reduction in renewables obligation certificate support if the economy struggles to provide such resources.

Strong investment in research is required to improve the competitiveness of renewable energy, but the proposed level of support for future large-scale commercial renewable energy generation through higher energy bills is questionable. Expensive energy is socially regressive and impacts on the poorest first and most affluent last. We should not forget that the end result of the Elizabethan transition from wood to coal was that energy became cheap and so human labour became expensive.

Nuclear Power Is the Cheapest Low Carbon Energy Source Available

Nuclear power is projected as being the lowest cost means of generating electrical energy, and by far the cheapest way to displace carbon from energy production. Our vast potential for offshore wind is projected to cost 15–21 p/kW-hr, onshore wind 8–11 p/kW-hr compared to 6–8 p/kW-hr for nuclear and 6–11 p/kW-hr for methane. These are levelised costs which include decommissioning for both nuclear and offshore wind, but do not include offshore connection costs. Published claims that Scotland can depend entirely on renewable energy are missing a thick appendix on costs. If we can deliver socially progressive low cost energy and environmentally progressive low carbon energy, then our transition to clean energy production will be far more likely. This is a no regrets policy.

Worryingly, some are actively disseminating plain disinformation concerning nuclear energy. Spurious claims are made that a nuclear plant has the same level of emissions as a methane-fuelled gas plant. This is simply untrue. For example, the full life-cycle carbon emissions of the Torness nuclear plant are only 7 gCO_2/kW-hr, similar to that of wind and less than 1% of coal at approximately 900 gCO_2/kW-hr. Similar disinformation can be found elsewhere. As a result of the 1974 decision to pursue nuclear energy, France brought on-line over 63,000 MW of nuclear power and now produces nearly 80% of its electrical energy from carbon-free nuclear plants. However, in their G8 Climate Scorecard the World Wildlife Fund for Nature (WWF) places France a lowly third. On reading the small print of their methodology it transpires that "WWF does not consider nuclear a viable policy option" and actual French carbon emissions for electrical energy generation are artificially inflated by a factor of

4 as a penalty, dropping France from clear first place to third. This is entirely unhelpful spin that would blush the cheeks of Malcom Tucker. The effective use of light water reactors in France, and elsewhere, shows the way forward for large-scale decarbonisation of an industrial economy.

Reducing Carbon Production Requires Improving Energy Density

If we're serious about displacing carbon from energy production we would be well advised to accelerate our journey along the historical path of improving energy density, away from coal and ultimately oil and towards methane and uranium. Methane has a carbon content about half that of coal and is easy to both store and transport. Due to its lower carbon content, methane offers perhaps a more realistic prospect for large-scale carbon capture. While many worry over, or in some cases naively welcome, the depletion of oil reserves, so-called peak oil, in future utilisation of low carbon methane is likely to grow as high carbon oil prices eventually rise. Hydrocarbon fuels will be with us for quite some time to come and casual talk of a post-carbon economy is entirely premature. It ignores the historical dynamics of the long waves of global energy transitions.

Previously unexploitable shale gas fields are now being tapped using technical innovations in seismic imaging and horizontal drilling to allow hydraulic fracturing of deep shale bedrock. Some predict that the world will be awash with shale gas in future. It will therefore be difficult for expensive renewable energy to compete with cheap methane if gas prices remain low for the long haul. Compressed or liquefied methane can be an almost direct substitute for oil in transportation using conventional internal combustion technology, and is particularly useful for fleet vehicles such as those used in public transport. Electric vehicles may also come to fruition once their high price and poor performance improves, but they will require a growing, reliable source of clean base-load energy for overnight charging.

Nuclear Energy Is Sustainable and "Recyclable"

Moving to higher energy density again, the use of nuclear fuels can grow significantly to offer energy for the deep future. Some dismiss nuclear energy as unsustainable since uranium is seen as a finite resource. This echoes Elizabethan agricultural writer Arthur Standish who bemoaned "there is no assurance how long they [coals] will last" at the beginning of the transition from wood to coal. In fact, nuclear energy has the almost magical quality that it can potentially breed its own fuel, while spent nuclear fuel (wrongly classified as waste) still has copious quantities of latent energy that can be extracted rather than buried.

Future so-called fast reactors, pioneered in Scotland at Dounreay, but now being aggressively pursued by China and India can convert this spent fuel into yet more clean energy leaving extremely small volumes of short-lived waste products. Contrary to received wisdom, spent nuclear fuel is a valuable asset. If we really must bury it, vitrification and deep geological storage are well understood, while the quantity of spent fuel is remarkably small. For comparison, each year a city-powering 1000 MW coal plant will dump 7.5 million tonnes of carbon dioxide as a gas directly into the atmosphere and produce approximately 400,000 tonnes of fly ash. An equivalent nuclear plant will produce 27 tonnes of spent fuel in solid form which can be easily separated from the environment, equal in volume to a box of . . . less than 3 [cubic] meters.

Through dogmatic opposition to nuclear energy, orthodox environmental thinking is blocking one of the most pragmatic and lowest costs means of displacing carbon from energy production. Compact base load nuclear plants are a direct substitute for base load coal plants. The sole result of historical opposition to nuclear energy has been that we have continued to burn more coal. Those who oppose nuclear energy should think carefully about the consequence of their actions. Simultaneously campaigning for firm action on climate change and against nuclear energy are entirely incompatible goals. The unseemly haste of Energy Minister Chris Huhne's recent and rapid conversion to nuclear advocacy was the result of being faced with the stark realities of real national energy and climate policy.

Nuclear Energy Is the Technology of Tomorrow

Nuclear energy is often claimed to be yesterday's technology. In fact, it is one of the key energy technologies of tomorrow. Future high temperature reactors can co-generate electricity and hydrogen for industry and transportation, or can desalinate seawater in developing nations. We have only scratched the surface of what is possible with energy dense uranium, and later vast untapped global reserves of thorium to help deliver a genuinely sustainable supply of clean, high-grade energy. Thorium is virtually unknown outside the world of energy analysts but utilises a fuel cycle which has many advantages over uranium, producing abundant energy and small quantities of short-lived waste products. It offers a compact source of clean, dependable energy so enormous as to be essentially unlimited, but only if we have the will and ambition to exploit it. Peak uranium worriers should take note.

To deliver both a low carbon and prosperous Scotland we need to quickly dispense with dogmatic views on nuclear energy and so ensure a balanced energy policy which is based on methane and uranium with a measured and appropriate use of renewable energy. We will then turn the corner on carbon emissions when our historical journey towards fuels of greater energy density overtakes growth in energy demand.

At present we are betting on renewable energy at any cost, economic or environmental, simply to eradicate nuclear energy from Scotland. We also need heretical greens who are prepared to challenge failed orthodox environmental thinking and embrace compact nuclear energy as the most effective means of decoupling human energy needs from the environment. It has a lower cost, a vastly smaller physical footprint and requires significantly less material than diffuse renewable energy. By any measure nuclear energy is green. Along with the growing use of methane, it represents one of the next waves in our long historical journey of energy transitions from Elizabethan-era forest and Victorian coal to cleaner fuels of greater energy density.

VIEWPOINT 

> *"Expanding nuclear power is not a sound strategy for diversifying America's energy portfolio and reducing global warming pollution."*

Nuclear Power Is Not a Sound Strategy to Fight Global Warming

Natural Resources Defense Council

In the following viewpoint, the Natural Resources Defense Council (NRDC) claims that the high start-up costs and planning time for new nuclear power plants repel investors unless there are government subsidy programs, and only large plants with a life span of twenty-five to forty years can be economically feasible. The NRDC rejects the argument that nuclear power is the most viable low-carbon energy source and claims that the growth rate of available wind power is higher. While remedies for issues such as a misappropriation of nuclear technology for weapons, the vulnerability of nuclear power plants to terrorist attacks, natural disasters, and waste disposal problems are theoretically possible, they are not yet available, according to the NRDC, and so nuclear power is currently neither secure nor environmentally responsible. The NRDC is an environmental action group.

Natural Resources Defense Council, "Nuclear Facts," February 2007. www.nrdc.org.

As you read, consider the following questions:

1. According to the viewpoint, what makes new nuclear power plants uneconomical compared to existing plants?
2. Compared to nuclear power, how much faster is wind power growing, according to the viewpoint?
3. According to the viewpoint, why do hotter summers affect nuclear reactors?

Until building new nuclear power plants becomes economically viable without government subsidies, and the nuclear industry demonstrates it can further reduce the continuing security and environmental risks of nuclear power—including the misuse of nuclear materials for weapons and radioactive contamination from nuclear waste—expanding nuclear power is not a sound strategy for diversifying America's energy portfolio and reducing global warming pollution. NRDC [Natural Resources Defense Council] favors more practical, economical, and environmentally sustainable approaches to reducing both U.S. and global carbon emissions, focusing on the widest possible implementation of end-use energy-efficiency improvements, and on policies to accelerate the commercialization of clean, flexible, renewable energy technologies.

The most economically efficient way to address the economic, environmental, and security risks of new nuclear power plants is to internalize the costs of avoiding or mitigating these risks in the market price of electricity and fuels. The United States can do this effectively by first regulating both carbon dioxide emissions and the unique risks posed by the nuclear fuel cycle, and then letting the "invisible hand" of the market deliver the lowest-cost technologies for providing energy services that meet minimum universal criteria for environmental sustainability, public health, and energy security.

The nuclear industry rejects this "level playing field" approach. Despite the public expenditure of some $85 billion on civilian nuclear energy development over the last half century, nuclear industry lobbyists continue to aggressively seek and obtain additional federal subsidies, so that investors in new nuclear power plants can earn a return on what would otherwise be a dubious commercial investment. Meanwhile, these subsidies displace government funding that could otherwise be directed toward cleaner, more competitive technologies with a much wider market potential for reducing global warming pollution. The fastest, cleanest, and most economical solutions to global warming will come if energy efficiency and renewable energy compete on a playing field that has been "leveled" by regulatory and taxation schemes that compel the pricing of polluting energy alternatives at closer to their true costs to society and the environment, not merely at their immediate costs of extraction and combustion.

Despite the fact that a national global warming emissions cap-and-trade system would materially assist the economic case for nuclear power, the nuclear industry has not been willing to openly advocate for such a system. This suggests either that the industry privately lacks confidence in its own rosy claims that nuclear energy can play a big future role in displacing carbon, or that large generating companies prefer that U.S. taxpayers shoulder the lion's share of the risk, while they harvest the carbon savings from new nuclear plants to prolong the profitability of their polluting coal-fired plants. Probably both explanations are true.

Subsidies Mask True Costs of New Large-Scale Nuclear Plants

Existing nuclear plants can compete favorably with fossil-fuel plants because they have relatively low operation, maintenance, and fuel costs, and their excessive capital costs have long since been forcibly absorbed by ratepayers and bondholders. But the continuing high construction costs of new nuclear power plants make them uneconomical. In fact, there have been no successful nuclear plant orders in the United States since 1973.

To jumpstart private investment in the first 6,000 megawatts (MW) of new nuclear power capacity, Congress granted roughly $10 billion in new subsidies—in the form of production tax credits, loan guarantees, federal "cost-sharing," and "regulatory risk insurance"—as part of the 2005 Energy Policy Act. The high capital cost of constructing an individual nuclear power plant has in the past dictated a trend toward ever larger reactor units in order to recoup the multi-billion investments required. At a price tag of $2.5 billion to $4.0 billion each, reactors typically require a long investment recovery period, on the order of twenty-five to forty years. Moreover, they usually require at least a decade or more to plan, license, and build, creating a persistent problem of economic "visibility" for nuclear reactor projects in what has now become a more competitive and shifting energy marketplace, at least in the United States.

The timescales involved in the current subsidy program illustrate the nuclear economic visibility problem. The Internal Revenue Service will distribute future annual production tax credits—nominally amounting over the first eight years of operation to a maximum of $1 billion for each thousand megawatts of new capacity—among all "qualifying" new nuclear reactor projects that have:

- applied for a construction/operating license from the Nuclear Regulatory Commission by the end of 2008;
- begun construction of the reactor building by January 1, 2014, and;
- received a certification from the Department of Energy that it is "feasible" to place the facility in service prior to January 1, 2021.

It is difficult to forecast today what energy market conditions will be like five years hence, much less in 2021. It is also difficult to predict the size of the subsidy ultimately available to each new reactor's owner, as this depends on the total number of projects that actually begin construction by 2014. How many ways will this gift from the taxpayers be divided before the commercial viability of each individual project is undermined?

Needless to say, absent favorable shifts in the underlying economic determinants of nuclear power, the addition of 6,000–9,000 heavily subsidized nuclear megawatts to the national grid beginning 10–15 years from now does not really diminish any of the immediate challenges posed by global warming, unless these plants actually replace existing or currently planned coal-fired power plants.

Renewable Energy Technologies Are Expanding Faster than Nuclear

It is instructive to compare this "nuclear renaissance" with the current rate of growth in wind power, which is adding about 3,000 MW of generating capacity per year. To accurately compare the two, capacity utilization must be factored in: Assuming a favorable case, namely that by 2021 the nuclear tax credits actually stimulate 1.5 times the amount of subsidized capacity, and with an average capacity utilization factor of 85 percent, then 0.85 × 9,000 MW = 7,650 MW/15 years = 510 MW/yr as the average annual expected growth for nuclear, but with none of it available for at least 10 years.

Even though wind has a much lower capacity utilization factor, and even assuming no further acceleration in its rate of growth, then 0.35 × 3,000 MW × 15 yrs = 15,750 MW for wind over the same period, or at least 1,050 MW/yr, with all of it available each year. In other words, windpower is already growing at twice the potential growth rate of nuclear over the next decade, and the outlook for wind is for even faster growth. In a similar vein, recent dramatic improvements in the processes for mass-producing solar photovoltaic cells suggest that by the time these subsidized new nuclear plants are connected to the grid, distributed solar power will be a formidable, and likely superior competitor.

Nuclear Energy Does Produce Carbon Emissions

An operating nuclear power plant has near-zero carbon emissions (the only outputs are heat and radioactive waste); it's the other steps involved in the provision of nuclear energy that can increase its carbon footprint. Nuclear plants have to be constructed, uranium has to be mined, processed and transported, waste has to be stored, and eventually the plant has to be decommissioned. All these actions produce carbon emissions.

Kurt Kleiner, "Nuclear Energy: Assessing the Emissions," Nature Reports Climate Change, *September 24, 2008. www.nature.com.*

Nuclear Capital Costs Remain Too High

If these subsidized "first mover" nuclear plants fail to produce major design and production innovations that significantly reduce the high capital cost of subsequent nuclear power plants—and there is little evidence to date to indicate that they will—then private investors will return to looking unfavorably on the industry once the current tax credits expire. The cost growth already occurring in the new Areva "European" power reactor under construction in Finland is not encouraging. The 2002 cost estimate of $2.3 billion for this 1,500 MW reactor had grown to $3.8 billion by July 2006, and this number does not include "off-balance-sheet" costs of €1.5–2 billion euros ($1.92–$2.56 billion) that reactor builder Areva has separately agreed to devote to the project.

A probable total project cost at or above $5 billion for this new reactor is certain to scare U.S. utilities and capital investors from making an aggressive commitment to nuclear energy in the near term. Moreover, as the technologies for renewables, energy efficiency, and industrial waste-heat regeneration continue to improve, they will become increasingly attractive investment alternatives to nuclear power.

A national cap on carbon emissions would certainly help reduce nuclear's significant current cost differential with large coal- and gas-fired power plants, but it will not ensure that nuclear stays competitive with these smaller, cheaper, cleaner, faster, and more flexible distributed sources of electric power generation.

The Security and Environmental Health Risks of the Nuclear Fuel Cycle Must Be Further Reduced

Although the nuclear fuel cycle emits only small amounts of global warming pollution, nuclear power still poses significant risks to the world. In a number of countries, peaceful nuclear materials and equipment have already been diverted to secret nuclear weapons programs, and could be again. Even worse, they are susceptible to theft by, or eventual sale to, terrorists or international criminal organizations.

Storage pools of spent nuclear fuel are likewise vulnerable to terrorist attacks that could disperse lethal levels of radioactivity well beyond the plant perimeter. The accidental release of radioactivity, whether from a reactor accident, terrorist attack, or slow leakage of radioactive waste into the local environment, poses the risk of catastrophic harm to communities and to vital natural resources, such as underground aquifers used for irrigation and drinking water. There are continuing occupational and public health risks associated with uranium mining and milling, especially in areas where such activities are poorly regulated. And underground repositories, meant to isolate high-level radioactive waste and spent fuel from people and the environment for thousands of years, are subject to long-term risks of leakage, poisoning the groundwater for future generations.

All of these problems have potential remedies, but most are not in effect today. For example, current international arrangements are insufficient to prevent a non-weapon state, such as Iran or Japan, from suddenly changing course and using nominally peaceful uranium enrichment or spent-fuel reprocessing plants to separate nuclear material for weapons. While long-term isolation of nuclear waste in stable geologic formations appears achievable technically, there is not a single long-term geologic repository for spent nuclear fuel in operation anywhere in the world.

Before nuclear power can qualify as a strategically and environmentally sound approach to reducing global warming pollution, the international nuclear industry, the respective governments, and the International Atomic Energy Agency must also ensure that:

- nuclear fuel cycles do not afford access, or the technical capabilities for access to nuclear explosive materials, principally, separated plutonium and highly enriched uranium;
- the Nuclear Nonproliferation Treaty[1] regulating nuclear power's peaceful use is reinterpreted to prohibit the spread of latent as well as overt nuclear weapons capabilities, by barring exclusively national ownership and control of uranium enrichment (or reprocessing) plants in non-weapon states;
- the occupational and environmental health risks associated with uranium mining and milling are remedied; and
- existing and planned discharges of spent nuclear fuel and other high-level radioactive waste are safely sequestered in geologic repositories that meet scientifically credible technical criteria for long-term containment of the harmful radioactivity they contain.

The Balance Sheet for New Nuclear Power

The Plus Side

- Very low emissions of carbon and other combustion-related air pollutants (but still some, from uranium mining, milling, enrichment, reactor construction-decommissioning, and waste management activities)
- Large, concentrated source of round-the-clock base-load power
- Low fuel costs compared to fossil alternatives
- If carbon emissions are effectively "taxed" at \$100-\$200 per ton under a carbon cap-and-trade system, nuclear might compete effectively with large coal-fired central station power plants

The Downside

- It's expensive low carbon power (\$0.9–\$0.10/kWh delivered) compared to \$0.025–\$0.030 for end-use efficiency improvements, \$0.06–\$0.07 for wind, and \$0.026–\$0.04 for recovered heat co-generation
- Long gestation/construction period and huge capital costs increase risk of market obsolescence and "stranded costs" (i.e., costs that cannot reasonably be recovered by continuing to operate the plant for its planned life)
- Subject to infrequent, but prolonged and costly planned and unplanned shutdowns (a recent study by the Union of Concerned Scientists documents 12 year-plus reactor outages since 1995, 11 of them "safety-related")
- Large "lumpy" increments of nuclear capacity require expensive overall power system excess capacity to ensure grid reliability
- Any nuclear power investment may at any moment become hostage to the conduct of the worst performer—or even the average performer on a bad day—in the event of a

reactor accident or near-accident anywhere on the globe

- No licensed path (yet) to opening first long-term geologic repository for safely isolating spent fuel, and nuclear "renaissance" will require either additional expensive and hard-to-establish geologic repositories, or even more expensive and hazardous spent-fuel reprocessing
- Nuclear security concerns and risks are heightened in an age of transnational terrorism
- Acute proliferation concerns arise if advanced fuel cycles are used, or if uranium enrichment capability spreads to additional countries that are not already nuclear weapon states
- All stages of the nuclear fuel cycle involve potentially harmful, or in some cases disastrous environmental impacts (e.g., Chernobyl [the 1986 meltdown at a nuclear power plant in Ukraine]), requiring continuous and vigorous regulation, with significant financial penalties exacted for poor environmental and safety performance to ensure compliance
- Huge heat dissipation requirements demand either large evaporative cooling withdrawals and/or thermal discharges into already overburdened lakes and rivers, or massive and expensive fan-driven air-cooling towers
- Climate change in the direction of hotter, drier summers spells trouble for reactors that rely primarily on cheaper once-through or evaporative water cooling
- Offer little prospect of increasing "energy independence," as the bulk of world uranium resources are located outside the United States

Note

1. The treaty, which went into effect in 1970, aims to prevent the spreading of nuclear weapons or weapons technology and to promote the peaceful use of nuclear power. The treaty has been signed by 190 parties, including the United States, Russia, Great Britain and France.

Viewpoint 

> *"We already have an energy source that is relatively cheap to use and that produces less environmental and public health impact than fossil fuels. That source is nuclear energy."*

Nuclear Power Is a Viable Source of Renewable Energy

Mario Salazar

In the following viewpoint, Mario Salazar argues that the dangers of nuclear power have been greatly exaggerated while those of other energy sources have been downplayed. Using a gas leak accident in Bhopal, India, as an example, he maintains that far fewer people have been harmed by the nuclear industry than by other industries and energy sources. Disaster scenarios, he says, do not acknowledge that, like all other energy sources, nuclear power is relatively safe and environmentally viable, given its low carbon emissions. In addition, Salazar contends that using breeder reactors rather than traditional reactors is a potential solution to the problem of nuclear waste disposal. Salazar is an environmental engineer and a former employee of the US Environmental Protection Agency.

Mario Salazar, "Nuclear Power: The Case for a Safe, Alternative Energy Source," *The Washington Times Communities*, December 28, 2011. http://communities.washingtontimes.com.

As you read, consider the following questions:

1. What does the author refer to when he claims that every energy source has built-in dangers?
2. According to the author, why is the 9/11 terrorist attack an argument in favor of the relative safety of nuclear power?
3. According to the author, what will happen in six hundred years?

We keep talking about the evils of fossil fuel and the promise of renewable energy, but we ignore the obvious. We already have an energy source that is relatively cheap to use and that produces less environmental and public health impact than fossil fuels. That source is nuclear energy. Until we are able to develop renewable sources of energy that are more efficient, it will remain the best alternative to coal and oil.

Nuclear Power Has Caused Fewer Deaths than the Fossil Fuel and Petrochemical Industries

Even if we consider the deaths caused by the bombs dropped on Hiroshima and Nagasaki [in 1945], the number of people killed by nuclear power since the middle of the last century is only a fraction of the deaths caused by fossil fuel and the petrochemical industry. Every day we read about gas explosions, car fires, and many other accidents in which fossil fuels were at least contributors. We hardly notice the deaths from cancer and lung disease caused by pollutants from burning fossil fuels.

We have become so jaded to these deaths that we hardly associate them with fossil fuels. In the rush to exploit these fuels, we also discount the possible dangers of ground water pollution from "fracking" [a method of extracting oil or natural gas] (as well as the problems associated with consuming vast amounts of water in drought-stricken regions that fracking requires), the potential for gas explosions, and other human and environmental risks.

Every energy source has built in dangers. Wind farms decimate migratory bird populations, corn ethanol drives up food prices around the world and consumes enormous amounts of water, and the production of solar cells also produces toxic waste. There's no such thing as safe energy, but only relatively safe energy. And nuclear energy is relatively safe.

Events like [the nuclear meltdowns at] Three Mile Island in Pennsylvania [in 1979], Chernobyl in Russia [in 1986], and Fukishima in Japan [in 2011] have been widely reported, but even these events did not cause the large number of deaths that the Bhopal[1] accident caused in India.

We didn't stop all chemical plants because of that. We made sure we implemented safer procedures. However, many people are still extremely afraid of nuclear power plants.

Fanning Public Fears of Nuclear Power

The media, in many cases without adequate knowledge, have helped to inflame opposition to nuclear power with scenarios that do not coincide with the technical state of the art or with safety features of new nuclear power plant designs. We all have seen movies in which a mad person takes over a nuclear plant or in which a terrorist explodes a nuclear bomb in one of our cities. While these scenarios are possible so is an asteroid strike that would wipe out all life on earth. Possibilities aren't all the same. You could win a power-ball lottery, but you'd be a fool to plan your life around the possibility. The logistics involved in creating one of these doomsday scenarios are extremely complex, and while we should build safeguards against their occurrence, they shouldn't dictate our decisions about nuclear power.

More feasible terrorist scenarios are the hijacking of a dozen tanker trucks to explode in an urban area, the poisoning of a city's water supply, or even the use of airliners to hit sky scrapers. There are "weapons of mass destruction" all around us, but they

Advantages and Disadvantages of Nuclear Power

Advantages

- Fuel is inexpensive
- Energy generation is the most concentrated source
- Waste is more compact than any source
- Extensive scientific basis for the cycle
- Easy to transport as new fuel
- No greenhouse or acid rain effects

Disadvantages

- Requires larger capital cost because of emergency, containment, radioactive waste and storage systems
- Requires resolution of the long-term high level waste storage issue in most countries
- Potential nuclear proliferation issue

"Comparison of Various Energy Sources,"
The Virtual Nuclear Tourist, *April 12, 2009.*
www.nucleartourist.com.

don't excite film makers the way nuclear terrorism does. Why? Because they don't have the fear value of nuclear disaster.

The number of recorded fossil fuel explosions (and their resulting death toll) over 120 years is too long to mention, but one terrorist scenario above happened on 9/11, and the explosive was jet fuel, not plutonium. Almost 3,000 people died when the planes hit the World Trade Center, the Pentagon and a field in Pennsylvania. The terrorists didn't need nuclear materials to destroy their targets, just flying gas cans and box cutters.

We have grown so accustomed to the great threats of fossil fuel products, both as energy sources and as the base of our petrochemical industry, that we no longer see them as a threat to our lives the same way we see nuclear power. This reminds me of the fear that many people have of traveling by airplane when the statistics show us that we have a better chance of dying from a car accident. We over estimate the risks of the unusual and underestimate the risks of the commonplace.

The Benefits of Fossil Fuels

Let's be clear, there is a place in our future for fossil fuels and petrochemicals. However, we should concentrate in using this limited resource in the production of durable goods and also implement a complete system of reuse and recycle. You can use "plastic lumber" to resurface a balcony in your home and after ten years it will look the same as the day you installed it. Burning or burying a resource that is limited does not make sense in a smart society. We already know of techniques to extend the benefit of fossil fuels and petrochemicals in ways that are smarter and kinder to Mother Earth and safer to us mortals.

So what are the real draw backs of nuclear plants? Beside the inflated fear of a nuclear disaster, most of the opposition to nuclear power comes from the disposal of used nuclear fuel. Serious discussions about the subject always end up with the question, "So what do we do with the spent fuel?"

Are Breeder Reactors a Solution to the Problem of Nuclear Waste?

The one solution most scientists appear to agree on is the use of breeder reactors [a reactor generating more fissile material, i.e. material maintaining a chain reaction, than it consumes]. However, there exists a number of challenges to this approach, and with the opposition to all things nuclear, many have put research of this option on the backburner. China is seriously looking at this option as a solution to its energy needs of the future.

Theoretically, breeder reactors could produce significantly less waste than traditional reactors.

Until a permanent solution is realized, we should depend on current techniques of disposal of nuclear materials such as the facility at Yucca Mountain in Nevada. Singling out a site like this is no different from, and probably much more environmentally benign, the hundreds of thousands of sites around the world where we have deposited the waste from the fossil fuels and petrochemical industries.

In fact it is easy to realize that our landfills today are full of plastics and other components of the fossil fuels and petrochemical wastes from our modern (disposable) way of life. How many times have you seen on TV that in 600 years one thing we can look forward to is the degradation of the first plastic bottle? Sad, but true.

Note

1. On December 2, 1984, methyl isocyanate gas leaked at a pesticide plant in Bhopal, India, killing an estimated 2,300 people immediately, and up to 8,000 in the years since.

Viewpoint 8

"Better . . . to take the huge amounts of money needed for nuclear plants and use it to build lower-cost solutions that will displace more coal."

Nuclear Power Does Not Compare to Other Renewable Energy Sources

Mark Clayton

In the following viewpoint, Mark Clayton reports that every energy source leaves a carbon footprint, yet that of nuclear energy production and renewable energy production is quite comparable and much better than that of fossil fuels. Once we consider cost-efficiency of energy production, Clayton observes, nuclear power falls behind renewable energies. Therefore, according to Clayton, many researchers argue that the huge amounts of money spent on new nuclear power plants would be better used in researching more cost-effective energy solutions that can replace coal. While nuclear power should not play a bigger role in the future, greener alternatives must. Clayton is a staff writer at the Christian Science Monitor.

Mark Clayton, "How Green is Nuclear Power?," *Christian Science Monitor*, March 7, 2007.

As you read, consider the following questions:

1. What does the industry say is entailed in its claim that nuclear power is carbon-free, according to Clayton?
2. According to the viewpoint, would improving energy efficiency reduce our carbon footprint?
3. What are, according to the author, the main arguments of environmental groups against nuclear power?

In Kansas, where winds blow strong, the push for clean energy includes not only new wind turbines but also new nuclear-power plants as part of a "carbon-free" solution to climate change.

It's an idea that may be catching on. At least 11 new nuclear plants are in the design stage in nine states, including Virginia, Texas, and Florida, according to the Nuclear Energy Institute website.

But that carbon-free pitch has researchers asking anew: How carbon-free is nuclear power? And how cost-effective is it in the fight to slow global warming?

Carbon-Free Energy Does Not Exist

"Saying nuclear is carbon-free is not true," says Uwe Fritsche, a researcher at the Öko Institut in Darmstadt, Germany, who has conducted a life-cycle analysis of the plants. "It's less carbon-intensive than fossil fuel. But if you are honest, scientifically speaking, the truth is: There is no carbon-free energy. There's no free lunch."

Nuclear power has more than just a little greenhouse gas attached to it, when mining uranium ore, refining and enriching fuel, building the plant, and operating it are included. A big 1,250 megawatt plant produces the equivalent of 250,000 tons of carbon dioxide a year during its life, Dr. Fritsche says.

That's still much less than coal-fired power plants and natural-gas turbines. It even does better than solar power and small-scale hydro projects. However, the gap with solar is closing and emissions from manufacturing photovoltaic panels are now on par with nuclear, a new study funded by the US Energy Department finds.

Officials in the nuclear power industry say references to carbon-free energy in their promotions refer only to the power-plant operation—and are not intended to describe carbon emissions during the entire nuclear life cycle.

Nuclear and Renewable Energy Sources Have Comparable Carbon Footprints

"Yes, absolutely there's carbon," says Paul Genoa, director of policy development for the Nuclear Energy Institute, which represents the nuclear power industry in the US. "Most studies have found life-cycle emissions of nuclear to be comparable with renewable. Some show nuclear to be extremely high, but we do not find those credible."

Neither do many researchers. A 2003 Massachusetts Institute of Technology study recommended vast expansion of nuclear power to make a dent in the climate-change problem. Princeton [University] researchers also cited it as an option, although they acknowledged concerns about terror threats and potential accidents.

One University of Wisconsin life-cycle emissions study in 2003 found even lower carbon emissions for nuclear than for most renewables. "We found wind and nuclear fission to have the lowest greenhouse-gas emissions over their life-cycle," says Paul Meier, director of the energy institute at the university. "We didn't include biomass and some of the others now available."

Yet it's not so much nuclear's carbon emissions, which are still relatively modest, but its cost-effectiveness in reducing carbon-dioxide emissions globally that's the key question, researchers say. Few studies have addressed that question.

Wind and Solar Power Are Better Alternatives than Nuclear

Nuclear power reactors are just boilers. Is it sensible to make plutonium and highly radioactive fission products just to boil water? . . .

Luckily, the world has a free thermonuclear reactor in the sky: the sun, which also animates the winds. Innovations in renewable resources make it possible to take nuclear power out of our energy future. Wind power . . . is cheaper than new nuclear power plants. Solar photovoltaics are expected to be cheaper than coal without carbon capture in less than a decade.

Arjun Makhijani, "The Fukushima Tragedy Demonstrates that Nuclear Energy Doesn't Make Sense," Bulletin of the Atomic Scientists, *July 21, 2011. www.thebulletin.org.*

Renewable Energy Offers More Bang for the Buck

According to one study that has studied the question, nuclear power may not fare as well when its life-cycle cost of reducing CO_2 emissions is compared with other energy alternatives. An Öko Institut study last year found that countries would get more bang for their buck by moving to other forms of energy—such as biomass and even some natural-gas power plants—rather than nuclear power.

Wind surprisingly has about the same carbon footprint as nuclear when manufacturing and load factors are included. But wind power also doesn't produce long-lived nuclear waste—storage of which includes an energy cost that's unknown and is not factored into the Öko or most other analyses—yet.

Just improving a nation's energy efficiency would produce far less CO_2 than a new nuclear plant (5 grams vs. 32 grams per kilowatt-hour), the study found. And it would do so at lower cost (4.8 cents vs. 5.2 cents per kilowatt-hour).

A handful of other studies show far higher life-cycle CO_2 emissions for nuclear than the Öko study. One Dutch researcher, for instance, finds that a vast expansion of nuclear power could deplete ore reserves and lead to a far higher level of energy use—and carbon emissions—from extracting uranium and refining it.

Mr. Genoa of the Nuclear Energy Institute dismisses the claim.

Greener Alternatives Will Play an Increasing Role in Energy Production

"The bottom line is that society needs to figure out how to get the energy it needs at the lowest possible social and environmental costs," he says. "Any reasonable researcher would recognize that renewable energy has a significant and increasing role to play. But by 2050, these will not supply even a small percentage of the worldwide electricity need. You have to get real about what is needed—massive amounts of energy on a massive scale."

But for those energy experts who have done life-cycle analysis of nuclear power, the big concern is that policymakers may be misled into believing that just because nuclear CO_2 emissions are low, the cost of nuclear as an option to address climate change would be a bargain. Better they say to take the huge amounts of money needed for nuclear plants and use it to build lower-cost solutions that will displace more coal.

We Need Cheaper and Safer Solutions

"It's easy to show that building more reactors makes climate change worse than it should have been," says Amory Lovins, chairman of the Rocky Mountain Institute, an energy think tank in Snowmass, Colo. "That's because a dollar put into new reactors gives two to ten times less climate solution for the amount of coal-power displaced than if you had bought cheaper solutions with the same dollars."

Environmental groups, too, are well aware of the conundrum surrounding the claim of carbon-free energy. Most of them maintain that nuclear is not the answer to climate change.

But their antinuclear arguments have centered on environmental damage from nuclear waste, potential accidents, and terror threats.

"First, nuclear was supposed to be too cheap to meter; now, they're framing it as a solution to climate change," says Erich Pica, director of economic policy for Friends of the Earth, an environmental group. "We hope this Democratic Congress will be skeptical of that claim."

Periodical and Internet Sources Bibliography

The following articles have been chosen to supplement the diverse views presented in this chapter.

Mark Clayton — "How Green Is Nuclear Power?," *Christian Science Monitor*, March 7, 2007.

Steve Connor — "Nuclear Power? Yes Please . . . ," *Independent*, February 23, 2009.

Peter Fairley — "Cleaner Nuclear Power?," *Technology Review*, November 27, 2007.

Eben Harrell — "Nuclear Batteries," *Time*, February 28, 2011.

Katherine Ling — "Nuclear Power Cannot Solve Climate Change," *Scientific American*, March 27, 2009.

Scientific American — "The Future of Nuclear Power," 2009.

Benjamin Sovacool — "Nuclear Power Is a False Solution to Climate Change," *Jakarta Post*, July 15, 2008.

Ralph Vartabedian — "US Nuclear Waste Problem Gains New Scrutiny," *Los Angeles Times*, March 23, 2011.

Brian Walsh — "Top 20 Green Tech Ideas: Modular Nuclear Power," *Time*, December 6, 2010.

Harvey Wasserman — "Nuclear Power's Green Grassroots Mountain Demise," *Huffington Post*, March 20, 2012.

Wired — "Inconvenient Truths: Get Ready to Rethink What It Means to Be Green," May 19, 2008.

Chris Woodyarn — "Nuclear Power Undermines Electric Cars' Green Image," *USA Today*, March 24, 2012.

Fareed Zakaria — "A Renegade Against Greenpeace: Why He Says They're Wrong to View Nuclear Energy as 'Evil'," *Newsweek*, April 12, 2008.

Chapter 3

Is Nuclear Power an Economical Source of Energy?

Chapter Preface

The reliable and ample flow of energy is vital for any economy. When the lights go out, everything stops. Government subsidies (payments to energy providers) regulate the cost of energy by keeping the prices to consumers below market level and/or reducing the cost to producers. "Identifying the real costs of competing energy technologies is complicated by the wide range of subsidies and tax breaks involved," says Diana Powers, reflecting a major source of contention in the debate surrounding the financial feasibility of various energy sources.

All energy sources receive government subsidies, yet not necessarily in equal amounts. According to the Environmental Law Institute, between 2002 and 2008 "the [US] federal government provided substantially larger subsidies to fossil fuels than to renewables. Subsidies to fossil fuels—a mature, developed industry that has enjoyed government support for many years—totaled approximately $72 billion over the study period, representing a direct cost to taxpayers. Subsidies for renewable fuels, a relatively young and developing industry, totaled $29 billion over the same period." Similarly, the Union of Concerned Scientists claims that, compared to renewable energies, the nuclear power sector in the United States receives a larger amount of subsidies in the form of direct financial support as well as tax breaks for research and development, the planning and building of reactors, and for decommissioning old reactors and storing nuclear waste:

> Subsidies were originally intended to provide temporary support for the fledgling nuclear power industry, but the promised day when the industry could prosper without them and power from nuclear reactors would be 'too cheap to meter' has yet to arrive. It is unlikely to arrive any time soon, as cost estimates for new reactors continue to escalate and the nuclear power lobby demands even more support from taxpayers.

Factoring in the heavy federal subsidies, claims that nuclear power is cost effective compared to renewable energy may be misleading. *Time* magazine's Michael Grunwald argues that by favoring the heavily lobbied nuclear industry, government subsidies might bring about a nuclear renaissance, but at the expense of alternative and potentially better energy sources. A subsidy shift away from funding fossil fuels in favor of a particular energy source would greatly influence the success of that alternative energy sector. Thus the IEA (International Energy Agency) holds that government support can bring about positive change:

> Energy subsidies—government measures that artificially lower the price of energy paid by consumers, raise the price received by producers or lower the cost of production—are large and pervasive. When they are well-designed, subsidies to renewables and low-carbon energy technologies can bring long-term economic and environmental benefits.

The authors of the viewpoints in this chapter examine whether nuclear power is cost-effective compared to other energy sources, whether new technologies could potentially increase the financial feasibility of nuclear power, and whether shifting subsidies from fossil fuels to renewable energy sources could level the playing field for alternative energy.

Viewpoint 1

> *"It is now evident that nuclear power development cannot keep up with the pace of its renewable energy competitors."*

The Steady Decline of the Nuclear Industry Demonstrates That Nuclear Power Is Not a Viable Alternative Energy Source

Mycle Schneider and Antony Froggatt with Julie Hazemann

In the following viewpoint, the authors argue that nuclear power development cannot keep up with the pace of its renewable energy competitors. The authors point out that the number of operating reactors in the world has declined. Given that many reactors are about to become too old to use and yet cannot be replaced immediately due to the long construction periods and immense start-up costs, they contend, the decline is likely to continue unless the life cycle of reactors is increased. The Fukushima disaster in Japan, the authors conclude, makes it much less likely that the acceptable

Mycle Schneider and Antony Froggatt with Julie Hazemann, "Executive Summary and Conclusions," *World Nuclear Industry Status Report 2012*, Mycle Schneider Consulting, July 2012, pp. 4–8. www.WorldNuclearReport.org.

age limit for functioning reactors will be raised. Mycle Schneider is an international consultant on energy and nuclear policy, Antony Froggatt is a European energy consultant, and Julie Hazemann is the director of EnerWebWatch.

As you read, consider the following questions:

1. According to the viewpoint, how long has renewable energy outpaced nuclear energy?
2. What did the German government decide after the Fukushima disaster, according to the authors?
3. What is the largest nuclear builder in the world, according to the viewpoint?

Four weeks after the beginning of the nuclear crisis on Japan's east coast, [nuclear meltdown at the Fukushima nuclear plant following an earthquake and tsunami on March 11, 2011] the situation at the country's Fukushima Daiichi power plant remains far from stabilized. The damaged reactors continue to leak radioactivity, and although it is impossible to predict the overall impact of the disaster, the consequences for the international nuclear industry will be devastating.

The present *World Nuclear Industry Status Report 2010–2011* was to be published at the occasion of the 25th anniversary of the Chernobyl disaster [fire and explosion at the Chernobyl Nuclear Power Plant on April 26, 1986] in Ukraine. . . .

Renewable Energy Outpaces Nuclear Energy

The report also includes the first published overview of reactions to the catastrophe in Japan. But developments even prior to March 11, when the Fukushima crisis began, illustrate that the international nuclear industry has been unable to stop the slow decline of nuclear energy. Not enough new units are coming online, and the world's reactor fleet is aging quickly. Moreover, it is now evident that nuclear power development cannot keep up with the pace of its renewable energy competitors.

Annual renewables capacity additions have been outpacing nuclear start-ups for 15 years. In the United States, the share of renewables in new capacity additions skyrocketed from 2 percent in 2004 to 55 percent in 2009, with no new nuclear coming on line. In 2010, for the first time, worldwide cumulated installed capacity of wind turbines (193 gigawatts [GW]), biomass and waste-to-energy plants (65 GW), and solar power (43 GW) reached 381 GW, outpacing the installed nuclear capacity of 375 GW prior to the Fukushima disaster. Total investment in renewable energy technologies has been estimated at $243 billion in 2010.

The Nuclear Industry Faces a Slow Decline

As of April 1, 2011, there were 437 nuclear reactors operating in the world—seven fewer than in 2002. The International Atomic Energy Agency (IAEA) currently lists 64 reactors as "under construction" in 14 countries. By comparison, at the peak of the industry's growth phase in 1979, there were 233 reactors being built concurrently. In 2008, for the first time since the beginning of the nuclear age, no new unit was started up, while two were added in 2009, five in 2010, and two in the first three months of 2011. During the same time period, 11 reactors were shut down.

In the European Union, as of April 1, 2011, there were 143 reactors officially operational, down from a historical maximum of 177 units in 1989.

In 2009, nuclear power plants generated 2,558 TWh of electricity, about 2 percent less than the previous year. The industry's lobby organization the World Nuclear Association headlined "another drop in nuclear generation"—the fourth year in a row. The role of nuclear power is declining steadily and now accounts for about 13 percent of the world's electricity generation and 5.5 percent of the commercial primary energy.

Nuclear Power Usage Has Been Declining for Many Years

Before Fukushima, a "nuclear renaissance" . . . seemed well underway, except for this point: Nuclear power, as a total of world energy supply, has been in steady decline for the past decade.

From 2000 to 2008, nuclear energy dropped from 16.7% to 13.5% of global energy production. . . . While nuclear energy production has steadily increased, its piece of the global electricity pie is shrinking compared to traditional sources such as coal and alternatives like wind and solar power.

Kevin Voigt and Irene Chapple, "Analysis: Fukushima and the 'Nuclear Renaissance' That Wasn't," CNN, April 11, 2011. http://edition.cnn.com.

In 2010, 16 of the 30 countries operating nuclear power plants (one fewer than in previous years due to the closure of the last reactor in Lithuania) maintained their nuclear share in electricity generation, while nine decreased their share and five increased their share.

The Number of Operating Reactors Will Decline

The average age of the world's operating nuclear power plants is 26 years. Some nuclear utilities envisage reactor lifetimes of 40 years or more. Considering that the average age of the 130 units that already have been closed is about 22 years, the projected doubling of the operational lifetime appears, rather optimistic. One obvious effect of the Fukushima disaster is that operating age will be looked at in a quite different manner, as illustrated by the German government's decision to suspend operation of all reactors over 30 years old immediately following the start of the crisis.

One scenario in this report assumes an average lifetime of 40 years for all operating and in-construction reactors in order to estimate how many plants would be shut down year by year. This makes possible an evaluation of the minimum number of plants that would have to come on line over the coming decades to maintain the same number of operating plants. In addition to the units under construction, leading to a capacity increase of 5 GW (less than the seven German units currently off line), 18 additional reactors would have to be finished and started up prior to 2015. This corresponds to one new grid connection every three months, with an additional 191 units (175 GW) over the following decade—one every 19 days. This situation has changed little from previous years.

Achievement of this 2015 target is simply impossible given existing constraints on the manufacturing of key reactor components—aside from any post-Fukushima effect. As a result, even if the installed capacity level could be maintained, the number of operating reactors will decline over the coming years unless lifetime extensions beyond 40 years become the widespread standard. The scenario of generalized lifetime extensions is getting less likely after Fukushima, as many questions regarding safety upgrades, maintenance costs, and other issues would need to be more carefully addressed.

With extremely long lead times of 10 years and more, it will be practically impossible to maintain, let alone increase, the number of operating nuclear power plants over the next 20 years. The flagship EPR [European Pressurized Reactor] project at Olkiluoto in Finland, managed by the largest nuclear builder in the world, AREVA NP, has turned into a financial fiasco. The project is four years behind schedule and at least 90 percent over budget, reaching a total cost estimate of €5.7 billion ($8.2 billion) or close to €3,500 ($5,000) per kilowatt.

The dramatic post-Fukushima situation adds to the international economic crisis and is exacerbating many of the problems that proponents of nuclear energy are facing. If there was no obvious sign that the international nuclear industry could eventually turn empirically evident downward trend into a promising future, the Fukushima disaster is likely to accelerate the decline.

Viewpoint 2

> *"There are already too few top-quality nuclear suppliers around the world. Reducing the number of suppliers will reduce competition and innovation over the long term."*

Abandoning Nuclear Power Would Threaten Economic Security Worldwide

Jack Spencer

In the following viewpoint, Jack Spencer advocates that Japan revive its nuclear power sector despite the Fukushima disaster because Japan has few natural resources and depends on nuclear power. Shutting down reactors means a 10 percent power shortage, which in turn means a 20 percent increase in electricity cost, which, Spencer warns, might stifle economic growth. According to Spencer, not reviving the nuclear industry would threaten Japan's leadership position in this sector, which would ultimately affect the US nuclear industry, which has close ties to Japan's manufacturers and suppliers. The nuclear sector in Japan should resume its course with a focus on oversight and safety, Spencer concludes, to prevent both power shortages and economic hardships worldwide.

Jack Spencer, "Japan's Nuclear Withdrawal: Bad for Japan, Bad for the US, Bad for the World," *Heritage Foundation Backgrounder No. 2622*, November 7, 2011. www.heritage.org.

Spencer is a research fellow in nuclear energy policy at the Heritage Foundation.

As you read, consider the following questions:

1. According to the author, why does Japan risk losing most of its nuclear power by summer 2012?
2. According to the author, why has Japan chosen nuclear power?
3. What was the total dollar amount of Japanese exports of commercial nuclear business in 2010, according to the viewpoint?

After an earthquake and tsunami caused equipment failures, meltdowns, and release of radioactive material at Japan's Fukushima nuclear plant in March [2011], there has been much discussion in the Japanese government and among the public about whether to continue production of nuclear power. While Japan's former head of government Naoto Kan (prime minister at the time the accidents occurred) aggressively pursued his country's withdrawal from nuclear energy, the new prime minister (since September [2011]), Yoshihiko Noda, has acknowledged its enduring role for Japan. He has not, however, endorsed new policy. Japan's official post-Fukushima energy policy is scheduled for release in summer 2012. Despite this lack of policy clarity, Prime Minister Noda has said that existing reactors would be brought back online as quickly as possible, that construction on reactors that began pre-Fukushima could continue, and that exporting nuclear technology would remain a priority. However, he also has stated that Japan should reduce its reliance on nuclear energy, and has been vague on policies regarding any new reactor construction.

Nuclear Power in Japan Today

Before the disaster in March, 54 nuclear reactors provided 30 percent of Japan's electricity. The Japanese government had planned on increasing that amount to 50 percent by 2030 with two new reactors that were under construction, 12 more planned reactors, and a used-fuel management strategy that included recycling used nuclear fuel, which was in the near-final stage of implementation. Today, only 11 reactors remain in operation, with work halted on other projects. Only one reactor has been restarted since Japan began shutting down nuclear plants for regular maintenance and post-Fukushima inspections. Japan's remaining operating reactors are all scheduled to be shut down for regular maintenance by next summer [2012]. Since reactors are generally not being restarted once they are shut down, Japan risks losing most or all nuclear power by that time.

Despite Prime Minister Noda's attempts to restart Japan's idled reactors in the near term and to revive its nuclear sector in the long term, considerable barriers remain. Perhaps most significant is the need to restore local support for bringing shut-down reactors back online. Recently, the mayor of a town about 60 miles from Tokyo became the first local leader to officially call for the decommissioning of a reactor that was shut down after Fukushima. From a practical standpoint, this lack of support is critical because local authorities must provide approval before specific plants can restart.

Local support for nuclear power is not completely eroded however. It remains somewhat strong within communities that host commercial nuclear power plants. A mayor from the western Japanese prefecture of Yumaguchi was recently re-elected while supporting the construction of a new reactor. Although Yumaguchi is far away from Fukushima, the fact is that nuclear reactor construction brings jobs and economic growth to the regions where they are built. However, support tends to wane in communities that lie just beyond those that host reactors. While their support is secondary, they remain influential in determining whether to restart shuttered reactors.

Safety Must Be the Nuclear Industry's First Priority

Regardless of the economic benefits, safety must come first. While the risk of a catastrophic accident is extremely small, the consequences are grave. The future of Japan's nuclear industry largely depends on the nuclear sector's success in restoring public confidence in nuclear technology. To date, Japanese industry and authorities are working to do just that. Foremost, Japan is going through a major reorganization of its regulatory agencies. The intention is to combine the Nuclear and Industrial Safety Agency (NISA) with the Nuclear Safety Commission (NSC), and to then place the newly formed agency beneath the jurisdiction of the Ministry of the Environment instead of under the Ministry of the Economy, Trade and Industry, which plays more of an advocacy role. Japan may want to consider going a step further by creating an independent safety agency.

More immediately, all plants are being put through a series of stress tests with strict enforcement of safety regulations. These tests include identifying explicitly which safety measure must be taken and precisely how it will be enforced. The actual reactor will also be subject to stress tests, as will other major plant components, including safety systems, to ensure that they can withstand multiple and simultaneous natural disasters. NISA and the NSC will review the results of these tests, which are to be completed by the year's end.

Economics Matter Too

Once the Japanese establish that their reactors can operate safely, they must consider the economic implications of shuttering existing reactors, and of rejecting new construction. Japan chose nuclear energy because the country lacks adequate natural resources to power its modern economy. Japan focused on nuclear energy to minimize its reliance on imports of natural gas, coal, and oil. Now that less than 20 percent of its nuclear resources remain online, it has been forced to begin importing billions of

The Fukushima Disaster Had Wide-Reaching Effects on International Trade

The Fukushima disaster . . . caused much direct damage. . . . Natural disasters are generally followed by "v-shaped" recessions, characterized by an immediate drop in production, followed by a quick recovery. Exports and production are harmed because disasters ruin infrastructure, reduce the availability of jobs, and destroy productive capital. Typically, this lasts for a few months. These consequences of the disaster affected other regions as well: the disaster caused supply chain disruption and flow losses. For example, the world market is largely dependent on some Japanese products such as electronics and cars; Japanese production of these goods was severely reduced after the disaster, affecting consumers and companies that relied on them.

G20 Summit, "Topic Area A: Managing International Trade Risks and Disasters in a Global Economy," 2011. http://munuc.org.

dollars' worth of fossil fuel. According to the Japanese government, fuel prices could increase by nearly $40 billion a year—$312 per person, and $770 per household.

Recovering economically from the March earthquake and tsunami will be very challenging for Japan in and of itself. Adding yet more barriers to that recovery by forcing the shutdown of a major source of affordable energy makes little sense. According to the Japan Center of Economic Research, shutting down all of Japan's nuclear plants over the next year will cause a 1.2 percent annual loss of GDP, which equates to ¥7.2 trillion ($94 billion) in annual losses. The Japanese government estimates that such an occurrence would result in a 10 percent power shortage and a 20 percent increase in electricity costs. Given that Japanese industry accounts for 40 percent of the country's electricity use, such increases would be extraordinarily harmful not only for industry but also for consumers who will see the costs passed down to them.

These losses could be much worse if Japan impatiently turns to renewable energy to replace nuclear. Despite the proclamations of former Prime Minister Kan that renewable energy should cost one-third of what it does today, and one-sixth by 2030, no existing evidence suggests that to be plausible. Solar energy costs about 60 cents per kilowatt hour in Japan as opposed to 6 cents to 8 cents for nuclear energy. A government policy forcing a replacement of nuclear energy with renewable would be economically devastating. Any savings that come to fruition will be the result of market forces and private innovation, not political decrees.

The uncertainty created by the threat of long-term, government-imposed energy shortages is already having an impact. Not knowing whether the government will allow old nuclear plants to come back online prevents utilities from making investments in new sources. Therefore, any less than allowing old plants to be restarted will result in the long-term power shortages that will likely force companies that produce and consume energy to leave Japan.

Abandoning Nuclear Power in Japan Affects Global Markets

This uncertainty is already translating into real-world losses for Japan that could threaten economic growth beyond its borders. While industries have patiently waited in the months following the earthquake and tsunami for power to be restored, they likely will not wait much longer if the government institutes policies that prevent adequate amounts of affordable energy to be brought online. Financial analysts believe that Japanese industry would leave Japan rather than deal with power shortages. As the world's fourth-largest economy and fifth-largest exporter and importer, this would not only make Japan's economic recovery more difficult, but would have a negative impact on the rest of the world. Power shortages would likely result in higher near-term prices for goods exported by Japan, such as chemicals, automobiles, and electronics. It would lead to lost markets for those items that Japan imports, such as raw materials, fuel, and machinery.

The situation will be worse for those companies that rely specifically on nuclear power, generated, for instance, by the Hamaoka nuclear plant in central Japan. The utility that operates that plant agreed in May of this year to shut it down at the Japanese government's request. The problem is that significant portions of Japan's automotive industry, such as Toyota, Honda, and Suzuki, rely on that specific plant for power. While the power could eventually be replaced, the slow process will increase costs. Japan's cars will cost more, making them less competitive.

No New Construction Could Mean No Exports

Though Japanese exports of commercial nuclear business totaled just around $200 million last year [2010], the prospects for multibillion dollar projects around the world has attracted significant Japanese investment. Indeed, three of the handful of major nuclear suppliers around the world are Japanese. However, future decisions to forgo new domestic nuclear energy projects could undermine this investment opportunity. Whether legitimate or not, questions will be raised about why Japan deems its reactors unsafe for domestic use but acceptable for export.

The concerns are real, and will increase over time. A Japanese company's ability to compete internationally will likely diminish as its domestic projects close down. The U.S. nuclear industry provides a case in point: It no longer dominates the global commercial nuclear industry as it did when it was building new nuclear plants in the 1970s and 1980s. It has been replaced by companies from countries that have the most recent experience with new nuclear construction—like Japan. France is another strong example. It is a nation that has made domestic nuclear-fuel reprocessing a centerpiece of its spent-fuel management strategy and is now the global leader in spent-fuel-management services. If Japan puts an end to new nuclear projects, it will cede its position as a leader in nuclear construction.

This will not only hurt the Japanese economy, but the U.S. economy as well. There are already too few top-quality nuclear suppliers around the world. Reducing the number of suppliers will reduce competition and innovation over the long term. It will also have near-term repercussions. America's primary nuclear companies have developed strong relationships with their Japanese counterparts in order to increase their competitiveness. A strong Japanese nuclear export sector directly benefits American companies. If Japan's industry weakens, so might its U.S. counterparts.

A Japanese Decision Must Include Safety Reform and Commercial Leadership

The decision about how, or whether, to pursue nuclear energy is for Japan to make. However, a rational analysis that considers the safety record of nuclear power in its totality, and the economic implications of rejecting it, should move the Japanese government on a path of continued use. Of course, it should not do so blindly or without substantial reforms.

Japan must understand completely what allowed the Fukushima accident to happen. Despite the earthquake and tsunami, those reactors should have been shut down safely. There is never an excuse for the massive release of radiation that occurred there. As Japan fully learns the lessons of Fukushima, it must institute reforms to ensure that the mistakes of Fukushima are never repeated. Japan should not only seek answers internally, but also draw from international best practices. Lastly, it must institute regulatory reforms that correctly align authorities and responsibilities, including establishing a truly independent safety regulatory agency. Once reform is complete, it is time for Japan to restore its position of commercial nuclear technology leadership. It is important not only for Japan—but for the rest of the world, too.

VIEWPOINT 3

"Nuclear power is environmentally safe, practical and affordable. It is not the problem—it is one of the solutions."

Nuclear Power Is Cost Competitive with Other Forms of Energy

Ferdinand E. Banks

In the following viewpoint, Ferdinand E. Banks argues that renewable energies will be an increasing part of the energy mix, but they are too unreliable to replace nuclear power. Wind power, for example, runs at maximum efficiency only a third of the time, according to the author. Banks maintains that the low carbon emissions of nuclear plants offset the issue of nuclear waste. France, the country with the highest percentage of nuclear power, produces only one third of the per-person average of carbon dioxide of the United States, Banks notes. Cost comparisons of nuclear, coal, and gas continuously show, he maintains, that nuclear energy is the cheapest energy source per kilowatt-hour. Banks is an economist and former professor at Uppsala University.

Ferdinand E. Banks, "The Economics of Nuclear Power," *Energy Tribune*, April 1, 2010. www.energytribune.com.

As you read, consider the following questions:

1. What is the cost-benefit trade-off the author mentions?
2. What is the capacity factor, according to the viewpoint?
3. What, according to the author, offsets government subsidies in Sweden?

I would like to begin this brief exposition with a fairy tale that was corrected by two well-known "green" [those advocating environmentally friendly practices] energy promoters, Amory Lovins and Joseph Romm, and published in *Foreign Affairs* (1992), which is the prestigious journal of the Council on Foreign Relations. It goes like this:

> For example, the Swedish State Power Board found that doubling electric efficiency, switching generators to natural gas and biomass fuels and relying upon the cleanest power plants would support a 54 per cent increase in real GNP from 1987 to 2010—while phasing out all nuclear power. Additionally, the heat and power sector's carbon dioxide output would fall by one-third, and the costs of electrical services by nearly $1 billion per year. Sweden is already among the world's most energy-efficient countries, even though it is cold, cloudy and heavily industrialized. Other countries should be able to do better.

Renewables Are Supplements

I called that statement completely wrong the first time I saw it, while in my new energy economics textbook (2007) I suggest that it and similar contributions are misleading bunkum. For example, there are a number of questions that must be answered in detail before biomass can unambiguously be classified a large-scale fuel of choice for the near or distant future. As for renewables such as solar and wind, they will undoubtedly increase in quantity, but it will not be at the expense of nuclear.

As David Schlageter pointed out in *EnergyPulse* (2008), "Renewable energy sources only supplement the electric grid with intermittent power that rarely matches the daily electrical demand." He continues by saying that "In order for an electric system to remain stable, it needs large generators running 24/7 to create voltage stability. Wind and solar generation are not on-line when needed to meet energy demand and therefore to help decrease system losses." In the promised land of wind energy, Denmark, voltage stability is attained by drawing on the energy resources of Sweden and Germany (and perhaps Norway). The Danes pay for the imported electricity, but not for the stability—which they would do in the great world of economic theory.

Every member of the nuclear booster club, to include myself, should make it his or her business to memorize the quotations in the previous paragraph, because they provide an excellent contradiction to the tiresome delusion that it is economically feasible to largely supplant nuclear energy with renewables. They also suggest why—with electric demand on the verge of increasing faster than supply in many parts of the world—more nuclear capacity is now scheduled for introduction than at any time during the past 3 decades.

For those readers who have been exposed to secondary school algebra, the above reference to things like voltage stability is superfluous. Sweden and Norway produce, on the average, the lowest cost electricity in the world. Norway, however, generates almost all its electricity with hydro, which is generally recognized as the lowest-cost power source, while Swedish electricity is produced in almost equal amounts by hydro and nuclear. As I show in my forthcoming energy book (written with a Chinese scholar), with this as a background, elementary algebra indicates that the unit cost of Swedish nuclear power is equal to the unit cost of Norwegian (and Swedish) hydro. This is not a welcome conclusion for many pseudo-scholars.

Nuclear Energy Is Highly Competitive with Other Sources of Electricity

Since nuclear energy technology for large reactors is based on existing technology, the cost range [included in the Electric Power Research Institute's 2011 report] does not change in the 2015 to 2025 time frame. However, the analysis shows that nuclear energy is among the most competitive sources of non-carbon electricity even after other technology advances are taken into consideration.

Nuclear Energy Institute, "Nuclear Energy Is Competitive in Independent Cost Analyses of New Generating Capacity," Fact Sheet, September 2011. www.nei.org.

The Cost-Benefit Trade-off of Nuclear Energy

But what about nuclear waste, which is repeatedly portrayed as a malicious and unavoidable cost of nuclear based electricity because, ostensibly, it will have to be locked up for hundreds of thousands of years? An argument that is sometimes presented however is that the cost of disposing of nuclear waste is balanced by the benefit of no carbon dioxide emissions from nuclear facilities. For instance, the International Energy Agency (IEA) has calculated that for France—the country with the largest production of nuclear energy (as a per cent of the total output of electric power)—the average person is responsible for 6.3 tons of carbon dioxide, which e.g. is one-third of the US average.

The cost-benefit *trade-off* mentioned just above is probably worth remembering, however I prefer for students (and anybody else) to inform me that France intends to treat its 'waste' as a potential fuel, and to explain why. (A similar strategy has been proposed in the UK by their energy minister.) For that reason a law has been passed in France stipulating that toxic waste is to be stored in such a way that it can be comparatively easily accessed and recycled if, at some point in the future, technologies appear which will allow it to be used as a satisfactory input in the nuclear fuel cycle.

The latter provision is, as the reader might guess, partially intended to appease or possibly bewilder nuclear sceptics, because technology is already available for recycling this '*decnet*', [French for "waste"] and in the event that the price of newly mined and processed uranium escalates, it would almost certainly be utilized without further debate. Of course, as noted by many comments to *EnergyPulse*, few persons who work with or near uranium believe that there will be a shortage of this commodity in the foreseeable future, even if the forthcoming nuclear revival eventually assumed the dimensions of a Manhattan Project [nuclear research and development program that eventually produced the first atomic bomb].

Renewable Energy Is Unreliable

There are occasionally long discussions of the cost of nuclear relative to the cost of renewables in the technical literature. An item that frequently appears is the *capacity factors* of windmills and solar generators. In simple terms, the capacity factor gives the amount of energy (in e.g. kWh) that is actually obtained, as compared to that made available if maximum output (nameplate capacity × time) were realized. It appears that in the U.S. wind generation works at maximum efficiency about one-third of the time, but this is confusing. With capacity factors between 0.25 and 0.35, the energy actually obtained as a percentage of *maximum* energy is less than one-half for many long periods.

Nuclear Energy Is Cheaper

It might also be useful to cite some figures for the cost of nuclear relative to gas and coal. The *Economist* (July 9, 2005) presents estimates from several sources for average electricity costs. For German utilities the Union Bank of Switzerland (UBS) gives $0.015 per kilowatt-hour for nuclear, $0.031 to $0.038 for gas, and $0.038 to $0.044 for coal. Similarly, they give $0.017/kWh for nuclear in the US, $0.02 for coal, and $0.057 for gas. The International Energy Agency (IEA), employing a discount rate of 5%, argues that nuclear is $21 to $31/MWh, while gas ranges from $37 to $60/MWh. Other sources (e.g. Massachusetts Institute of Technology (MIT) and Britain's Royal Institute of International Affairs) disagree; however, I specifically make a practice of ignoring everything originating with the energy economists of [MIT] and the RIIA, especially the latter, and advise everyone reading this to do the same.

So much for cost, but what about price of nuclear electricity—especially to private enterprises and households? In the case of Sweden, the low cost of nuclear and hydro power, and fairly smart regulation, made it possible to provide electricity to the industrial sector at perhaps the lowest price in the world. This being the case, nothing is more offbeat than hearing about the subsidies paid [to] the nuclear sector. Cheap electricity meant the establishment of new enterprises, and just as important the expansion of existing firms. The tax income generated by these activities, and used for things like health care and education, more than compensated taxpayers (in the aggregate) for any subsidies that might have been dispensed by the government.

An antithetical situation may prevail for wind and biofuels. In Germany, the energy law guarantees operators of windmills and producers of solar energy an above-market price for power for as long as 20 years. This is an explicit subsidy, although it may be both economically and politically optimal due to the reduction in greenhouse gas emissions. More important, inexpensive electricity for plug-in hybrids is made available.

A more complex subsidy involves the exploitation of biofuels. Research newly carried in the United States, and reported in the influential journal *Science*, claims that almost all biofuels used today result in more greenhouse gas emissions than conventional fuels if the pollution directly and indirectly caused by producing these "green" fuels is taken into consideration. In addition, there would be a substantial loss of "consumer surplus" throughout the world due to a likely increase in food costs. Some of the intricacies of this important issue have been examined on an elementary level by Clay Ogg (2008).

France Goes Nuclear

In these circumstances, it might be argued that France's total acceptance of nuclear power makes a great deal of sense. As noted in the *Financial Times* (October 6, 2006), nuclear power has provided "an abundance of cheaply-produced electricity, made the country a leader in nuclear technology worldwide and reduced its vulnerability to the fluctuations of the turbulent oil and gas markets." France can also supply some electricity to neighbouring countries, which helps counterbalance the short sighted and unthinking foolishness being promoted by the European Union's directors and its Energy Directorate.

I know enough about electricity to have done work on power lines for the US Army during a brief period. And I have designed terminal installations for the US Navy. And while I have taught social science (i.e. economics) in 14 universities, I am still unable to understand why so many people are willing to risk the economic futures of themselves and their families because of the drivel being put into circulation by persons with a psychotic hatred of technological excellence, although they are quite capable of enjoying its material advantages. Something to be aware of here is that the rich will *never* be without reliable and plentiful energy, regardless of its availability or lack thereof to the less fortunate. One of the reasons that they will never be without it is that they are fully aware of its importance.

Perhaps the clearest argument for nuclear power has been presented by Rhodes and Beller (2000), which is similar to the basic contention of this article. They say that "Because diversity and redundancy are important for safety and security, renewable energy sources ought to retain a place in the energy economy of the century to come." The meaning here is clear, especially if you add that we probably will never possess what is known in intermediate economic theory as the optimal amount of nuclear power. But they do state that "nuclear power should be central. . . . Nuclear power is environmentally safe, practical and affordable. It is not the problem—it is one of the solutions."

> *"Energy efficiency and renewables are the key to affordable, carbon-free electricity. They should be a focus of national energy and climate policy. Not nukes."*

Nuclear Power Is Far More Expensive than Other Energy Alternatives

Joseph Romm

In the following viewpoint, Joseph Romm argues that nuclear power is too expensive to be cost effective. He explains that between 2000 and 2007, nuclear plant construction costs increased by 185 percent, and cites examples in North Carolina and Florida where costs even tripled. This cost makes investing prohibitive, Romm contends, unless investors recoup some of the costs from the consumer even before construction is completed. As he argues, this means that consumers pay for nuclear power long before they consume it. Other renewable energy sources, such as solar or wind, are more cost effective, he concludes, and energy efficiency could cut down demand and decrease consumers' carbon footprint. Romm is a US physicist and climate expert.

As you read, consider the following questions:

1. According to the author, is a nuclear renaissance likely in the United States?
2. Plant construction estimated to cost $4 billion in 2000 would have cost how much in October 2007, according to Romm?
3. California efficiency programs have, according to the viewpoint, cut the electricity demand by how much?

No nuclear power plants have been ordered in this country [the United States] for three decades. Once touted as "too cheap to meter," nuclear power simply became "too costly to matter," as the *Economist* put it back in May 2001.

Yet growing concern over greenhouse gas emissions from fossil fuel plants has created a surge of new interest in nuclear. *Wired* magazine just proclaimed "Go nuclear" on its cover. Environmentalists like Stewart Brand and James Lovelock have begun embracing nukes as a core climate solution. And GOP [2008 Republican Party] presidential nominee John McCain, who has called for building hundreds of new nuclear plants in this country, recently announced he won't bother showing up to vote on his friend Joe Lieberman's [U.S. Senator from Connecticut] climate bill because of insufficient subsidies (read "pork" [money set aside for a questionable purpose]) for nuclear power.

Nuclear Energy Is "Too Costly to Matter"

What do they know that scores of utility executives and the *Economist* don't? Nothing, actually. Nuclear power still has so many problems that unless the federal government shovels tens of billions of dollars more in subsidies into the industry, and then shoves it down the throat of U.S. utilities and the public with mandates, it is unlikely to see a significant renaissance in this country. Nor is nuclear power likely to make up even 10 percent of the solution to the climate problem globally.

Why? In a word, cost. Many other technologies can deliver more low-carbon power at far less cost. As a 2003 MIT [Massachusetts Institute of Technology] study, The Future of Nuclear Energy, concluded: "The prospects for nuclear energy as an option are limited" by many "unresolved problems," of which "high relative cost" is only one. Others include environment, safety and health issues, nuclear proliferation concerns, and the challenge of long-term waste management.

Since new nuclear power now costs more than double what the MIT report assumed—three times what the *Economist* called "too costly to matter"—let me focus solely on the unresolved problem of cost. While safety, proliferation and waste issues get most of the publicity, nuclear plants have become so expensive that cost overwhelms the other problems.

The Nuclear Industry Requires Heavy Subsidies

Already nuclear energy, the sequel, is a source of major confusion in the popular press. Consider this recent interview between *Newsweek*'s Fareed Zakaria and Patrick Moore, one of the co-founders of Greenpeace [organization advocating environmental sustainability], who is now a strong advocate for nuclear power. Zakaria asks, "A number of analyses say that nuclear power isn't cost competitive, and that without government subsidies, there's no real market for it." Moore replies:

> That's simply not true. Where the massive government subsidies are is in wind and solar . . . I know that the cost of production of electricity among the 104 nuclear plants operating in the United States is 1.68 cents per kilowatt-hour. That's not including the capital costs, but the cost of production of electricity from nuclear is very low, and competitive with dirty coal. Gas costs three times as much as nuclear, at least. Wind costs five times as much, and solar costs ten times as much.

In short: That's absurd. Nuclear power, a mature industry providing 20 percent of U.S. power, has received some $100 billion in U.S. subsidies—more than three times the subsidies of wind and solar, even though they are both emerging industries. And how can one possibly ignore the capital costs of arguably the most capital-intensive form of energy? Moore's statement is like saying "My house is incredibly cheap to live in, if I don't include the mortgage."

Plant Construction Costs Have Increased Dramatically

Furthermore, after capital costs, wind power and solar power are pretty much free—nobody charges for the breeze and the sun. Operation is also cheap, compared with nukes, which run on expensive uranium and must be monitored minute by minute so they don't melt down. Moore is talking about old nuclear plants, which have been paid off. But the price of new nuclear power has risen faster than any other form of power, as a detailed study of coal, gas, wind and nuclear power capital costs by Cambridge Energy Research Associates concluded.

In fact, from 2000 through October 2007, nuclear power plant construction costs—mainly materials, labor and engineering—have gone up 185 percent! That means a nuclear power plant that would have cost $4 billion to build in 2000 would have cost more than $11 billion to build last October [2007].

You know an industry is starting to price itself out of business when one of its trade magazines, *Nuclear Engineering International*, headlines a recent article "How Much? For Some Utilities, the Capital Costs of a New Nuclear Power Plant Are Prohibitive."...

As the article related, in 2005 the U.S. Energy Information Administration projected about $2,000 per kilowatt for a nuclear plant's "overnight capital costs"—the industry's rosy-eyed terminology for the cost of the plant if it could be built overnight, absent interest and financing costs, and assuming no construction cost overruns. At the time, Marvin Fertel, the chief nuclear officer at the Nuclear Energy Institute (NEI), told the Senate that the assumptions made on new nuclear plant construction were "unrealistically high and inflated."

But by mid-2007, a Keystone report funded in part by the nuclear industry and NEI estimated overnight costs at $3,000 per kilowatt, which, with interest, equals $3,600 to $4,000 per kilowatt. The report notes, "The power isn't cheap: 8.3 to 11.1 cents per kilowatt hour." That's not cheap, when you consider that in December 2007, retail prices in this country averaged 8.9 cents per kilowatt-hour.

Mid-2007 had already become the good old days for affordable nuclear power. Jim Harding, who was on the Keystone Center panel and was responsible for its economic analysis, e-mailed me in May that his current "reasonable estimate for levelized cost range . . . is 12 to 17 cents per kilowatt hour lifetime, and 1.7 times that number [20 to 29 cents per kilowatt-hour] in first year of commercial operation."

At the end of August 2007, American Electric Power CEO Michael Morris said that because of construction delays and high costs, the company wasn't planning to build any new nuclear plants. Also, builders would have to queue for certain parts and face "realistic" costs of about $4,000 a kilowatt. "I'm not convinced we'll see a new nuclear station before probably the 2020 timeline," Morris said.

Sky-High Start-up Costs Deter Investors

So much for being a near-term, cost-effective solution to our climate problem. But if $4,000 per kilowatt was starting to price nuclear out of the marketplace, imagine what prices 50 percent to 100 percent higher will do.

In October 2007, Florida Power and Light (FPL), "a leader in nuclear power generation," presented its detailed cost estimate for new nukes to the Florida Public Service Commission.

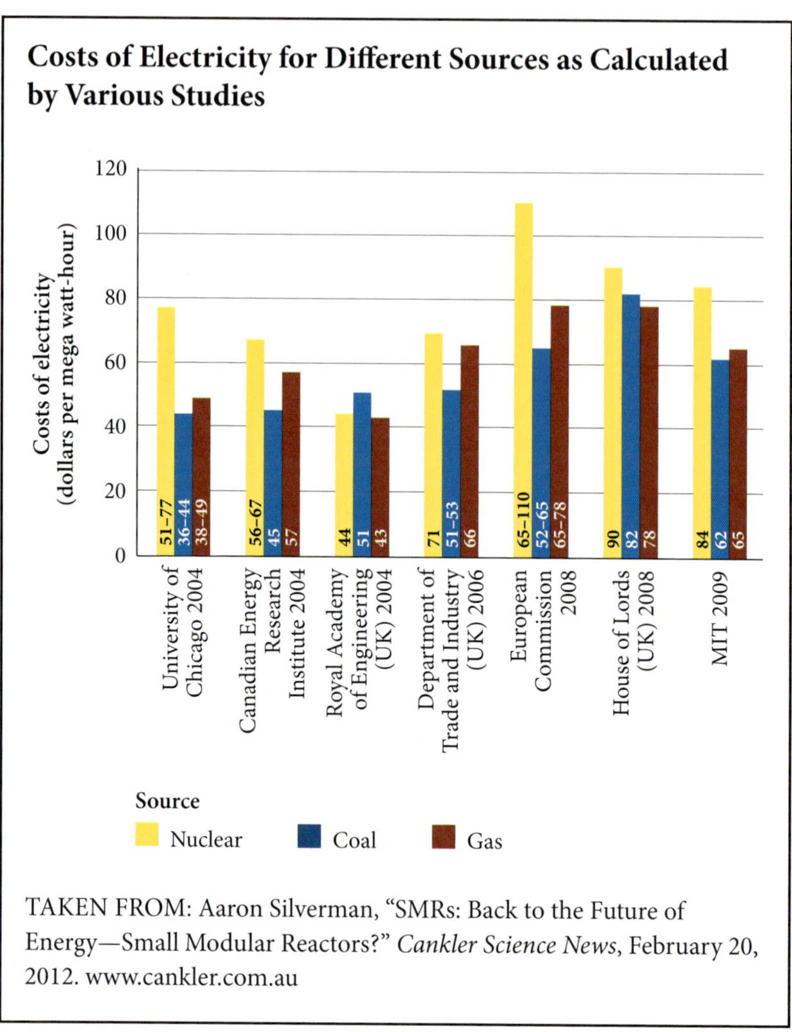

Costs of Electricity for Different Sources as Calculated by Various Studies

TAKEN FROM: Aaron Silverman, "SMRs: Back to the Future of Energy—Small Modular Reactors?" *Cankler Science News*, February 20, 2012. www.cankler.com.au

It concluded that two units totaling 2,200 megawatts would cost from $5,500 to $8,100 per kilowatt—$12 billion to $18 billion total!

Lew Hay, chairman and CEO of FPL, said, "If our cost estimates are even close to being right, the cost of a two-unit plant will be on the order of magnitude of $13 to $14 billion. That's bigger than the total market capitalization of many companies in the U.S. utility industry and 50 percent or more of the market capitalization of all companies in our industry with the exception of Exelon." This, he said, "is a huge bet for any CEO to take to his or her board."

In January, MidAmerican Nuclear Energy Co. said prices were so high it was ending its pursuit of a nuclear power plant in Payette County, Idaho, after spending $13 million researching its economic feasibility. Company president Bill Fehrman said, "Consumers expect reasonably priced energy, and the company's due diligence process has led to the conclusion that it does not make economic sense to pursue the project at this time."

MidAmerican is owned by famed investor Warren Buffett. When Buffett pulls the plug on a potential investment after spending $13 million analyzing the deal, that should give everyone pause.

Reactor Cost in North Carolina Is Deemed a Trade Secret

How expensive have nuclear plants become? So expensive that Duke Power has been refusing to reveal cost estimates for a nuclear plant for the Carolinas, saying it would reveal trade secrets. I kid you not. The *Charlotte News and Observer* reported in April [2008], "'If Duke is requested to disclose the cost today, it will undermine the company's ability to get the lowest cost for its customers,' said Duke attorney Lawrence Somers. 'In light of the testimony today, the public advocacy groups want the cost of this plant to go up.'"

Yes, those annoying public advocacy groups want to know the cost to the public of the plants before supporting them. The company actually testified that if everyone knew the plant's cost, that would "give tactical advantage to vendors and contractors during sensitive negotiations." What Duke seems to be saying is that if suppliers knew just how incredibly expensive the plant is, they would want a bigger piece of the pie. Such is the state of our free-market energy economy today.

Amazingly, North Carolina regulators agreed with Duke that the estimated cost is a "trade secret" under state law. South Carolina's consumer advocate, C. Dukes Scott, took a stance that was once called common sense in this country: "If you want the ratepayers to pay for something, are you going to tell them it's none of their business?"

In fact, back in February, Duke Energy CEO Jim Rogers told state regulators the plant would cost $6 billion to $8 billion, but a mere two months later said that estimate was "dated and inaccurate." Scott wondered, "If the cost wasn't confidential in February, how is it confidential in April?"

Reactor Cost in Florida Tripled

Let's take a look at one more example. Earlier this year, Progress Energy informed state regulators that the twin 1,100-megawatt plants it intends to build in Florida would cost $14 billion, which "triples estimates the utility offered little more than a year ago." That would be more than $6,400 a kilowatt. But wait, that's not all. As reported by the St. Petersburg Times, "The utility said its 200-mile, 10-county transmission project will cost $3-billion more." If we factor that cost in, the price would be $7,700 a kilowatt.

Amazingly, the utility won't even stand behind the exorbitant tripled cost for the plant. In its filing with state regulators, Progress Energy warned that its new $17 billion estimate for its planned nuclear facility is "nonbinding" and "subject to change over time."

And it gets even better (by I which I mean, worse) for Florida ratepayers. Florida passed a law that allows utilities to recoup some costs while a nuclear plant is under construction. How much? About $9 a month starting as early as next year! Yes, the lucky customers of Progress Energy get to each pay more than $100 a year for years and years and years before they even get one kilowatt-hour from these plants.

This would seem to be the exact opposite of the old claim for the nuclear industry, "Too cheap to meter." Now it's so expensive the company raises your rates before the power even gets to the meter!

Other Forms of Carbon-Free Power Are Cheaper than Nuclear

How the renewable industry would love to charge people before they built their plants. Even without that benefit, Jigar Shah, chief strategy officer of SunEdison, explained to me that he could guarantee delivery to Florida of more kilowatt-hours of power with solar photovoltaics—including energy storage so the power was not intermittent—for less money than the nuke plants cost.

Many other forms of carbon-free power are already cheaper than nuclear today, including wind power, concentrated solar thermal power and, of course, the cheapest of all, energy efficiency. Over the past three decades, California efficiency programs have cut total electricity demand by about 40,000 gigawatt hours for an average 2 to 3 cents per kilowatt-hour. A May [2008] presentation of modeling results by the California Public Utilities Commission shows that it could more than double those savings by 2020.

If California's effort were reproduced nationwide, efficiency would deliver 130 gigawatts by 2020, which is more than enough energy savings to avoid the need to build any new power plants through 2020 (and beyond). And that means any new renewable plants built could displace existing fossil fuel plants and begin to reduce U.S. carbon dioxide emissions from the utility sector.

A May [2008] report by the [US president George W.] Bush Energy Department concluded that Americans could get 300 gigawatts of wind by 2030 at a cost of 6 to 8.5 cents per kilowatt-hour including the cost of transmission to access existing power lines. And the cost of integrating the variable wind power into the U.S. grid would be under 0.5 cents per kilowatt-hour. (Wind turbines provide energy on average 35 percent of the time. Nukes average 90 percent availability. That means it takes 300 gigawatts of wind capacity to deliver as much electricity as about 120 gigawatts of nuclear.)

Finally we have the reemergence of concentrated solar thermal power (also known as concentrated solar power, or CSP). Utilities in the Southwest are already contracting for power at 14 to 15 cents per kilowatt-hour. The modeling for the California Public Utilities Commission puts solar thermal at around 13 cents per kilowatt-hour. Because CSP has large cost-reduction opportunities from economies of scale and the manufacturing learning curve, the modeling foresees the possibility that CSP costs could drop an additional 20 percent by 2020. And those prices include six hours of storage capacity, which allows CSP to follow the electric load, and that is even better than nuclear power, which is constant around the clock.

There Is No Need for a Nuclear Renaissance

All of these sources of electricity are considerably cheaper than the electricity that would be generated by new nuclear plants, which the commission estimates costs more than 15 cents per kilowatt-hour before transmission and delivery costs. This entire discussion doesn't even consider the issue of uranium supply, whose price has risen sharply in recent years. A big shift toward nuclear power would no doubt further increase prices. If, as many advocates want, we ultimately go toward reprocessing of spent fuel, that would add an additional 1.5 to 3 cents per kilowatt-hour to the cost of nuclear power.

Sen. McCain keeps saying, "If France can produce 80 percent of its electricity with nuclear power, why can't we?" Wrong question, Senator. The right question is: Why would we? Energy efficiency and renewables are the key to affordable, carbon-free electricity. They should be a focus of national energy and climate policy. Not nukes.

> *"A new type of nuclear reactor . . . is emerging as a contender to reshape the nation's resurgent nuclear power industry."*

Small Reactors Generate Big Hopes

Rebecca Smith

In the following viewpoint, Wall Street Journal *reporter Rebecca Smith discusses the advantages of small modular reactor designs, such as lower cost and shorter construction periods. In addition, notes Smith, smaller reactors do not have to be water cooled, and therefore do not have to be near water, which is often near heavily-populated areas. Most importantly, Smith reports, small modular reactors offer the opportunity to start with one module and add on later. Therefore, Smith concludes, small modular reactors are affordable even for smaller customers, while still offering safe energy production.*

As you read, consider the following questions:

1. What percentage of the nation's electricity is produced by nuclear power?

Rebecca Smith, "Small Reactors Generate Big Hopes," *Wall Street Journal*, February 18, 2010.

2. When will the next wave of large reactors go on line?
3. What idea drove the design of the Babcock & Wilcox reactor design?

A new type of nuclear reactor—smaller than a rail car and one tenth the cost of a big plant—is emerging as a contender to reshape the nation's resurgent nuclear power industry.

Three big utilities, Tennessee Valley Authority, First Energy Corp. and Oglethorpe Power Corp., on Wednesday signed an agreement with McDermott International Inc.'s Babcock & Wilcox subsidiary, committing to get the new reactor approved for commercial use in the U.S.

Although none have agreed to buy a reactor, the utilities' commitment should help build momentum behind the technology and hasten its adoption across the industry. It's a crucial first step toward getting the reactor design certified by the Nuclear Regulatory Commission. Early support from the three utilities, and four others that are mulling the agreement, increases the odds that customers will come forward in the future.

The news comes just as President Barack Obama announced more than $8 billion in loan guarantees this week that would pave the way for the first nuclear power plant in the U.S. in almost thirty years. He has proposed accelerating nuclear development by tripling the amount of federal loan guarantees for reactor construction to $54 billion.

The smaller Babcock & Wilcox reactor can generate only 125 to 140 megawatts of power, about a tenth as much as a big one. But the utilities are betting that these smaller, simpler reactors can be manufactured quickly and installed at potentially dozens of existing nuclear sites or replace coal-fired plants that may become obsolete with looming emissions restrictions.

"We see significant benefits from the new, modular technology," said Donald Moul, vice president of nuclear support for First Energy, an Ohio-based utility company.

He said First Energy, which operates four reactors at three sites in Ohio and Pennsylvania, has made no decision to build any new reactor and noted there's "a lot of heavy lifting to do to get this reactor certified" by the NRC for U.S. use.

Indeed, the smaller reactors still could incite major opposition. They face the same unresolved issues of where to put the waste and public fear of contamination, in the event of an accident. They could also raise alarms about creating possible terrorism targets in populated areas.

Still, the sudden interest in small reactors illustrates a growing unease with the route that nuclear power has taken for half a century. What many regard as the first commercial reactor built in the U.S., in 1957 at Shippingport, Pa., was only about 60 megawatts in size. By the time construction petered out three decades later, reactors had grown progressively bigger, ending up at about 1,000 megawatts of capacity.

Now, after a two-decade lull in construction, the U.S. is gearing up for a robust revival of nuclear power. Expanding the nuclear sector, which currently produces 20% of the nation's electricity, is considered essential to slashing carbon emissions.

Companies such as NRG Energy Inc., Duke Energy Corp. and Southern Co. are planning large reactors that cost up to $10 billion apiece and can generate enough electricity to power a city the size of Tulsa, Okla.

But there is growing investor worry that reactors may have grown so big that they could sink the utilities that buy them. An increasingly global supply chain for big reactors also worries investors.

"We think the probability that things will go wrong with these large projects is greater than the probability that things will go right," said Jim Hempstead, senior vice president at Moody's Investors Service. He warns that nuclear-aspiring utilities with "bet the farm" projects face possible credit downgrades.

The large price tag has begun to spook some utility executives. John Rowe, the chief executive of Exelon Corp.,

The Case for Small Modular Nuclear Reactors

SMRs [small modular reactors] have a number of advantages over conventional reactors. For one thing, SMRs are cheaper to construct and run. This makes them very attractive to poorer, energy-starved countries; small, growing communities that don't require a full-scale plant; and remote locations such as mines or desalination plants. Part of the reason for this is simply that the reactors are smaller. Another is that, not needing to be custom designed in each case, the reactors can be standardized and some types built in factories that are able to employ economies of scale. . . . Factory construction also allows SMRs to be built, delivered to the site, and then returned to the factory for dismantling at the end of their service lives—eliminating a major problem with old conventional reactors, i.e. how to dispose of them.

SMRs also enjoy a good deal of design flexibility. Conventional reactors are usually cooled by water—a great deal of water—which means that the reactors need to be situated near rivers or coastlines. SMRs, on the other hand, can be cooled by air, gas, low-melting point metals or salt. This means that SMRs can be placed in remote, inland areas where it isn't possible to site conventional reactors.

David Szondy, "Small Modular Nuclear Reactors—the Future of Energy," Gizmag, *February 16, 2012. www.gizmag.com*

which operates the nation's largest fleet of nuclear plants, had hoped to build a new reactor in Texas. But, having failed to get federal loan guarantees, he recently said he's having second thoughts.

Instead, his company is expanding the capacity of its existing nuclear plants and is looking at Babcock & Wilcox's design. Amir Shakarami, Exelon's senior vice president, said mPower provides "an alternative that is practical and scalable," offering a way to add zero-emission power in small amounts and avoid the rate shocks that accompanied big reactors in the past.

Already, the high cost of large reactors is generating friction among partners. CPS Energy and NRG Energy Inc. sued each other recently when CPS, a city-owned utility in San Antonio got cold feet about investing in a new nuclear plant that could push up power costs for its customers. . . .

The two agreed Wednesday to a settlement in which NRG will pay CPS $1 billion to reduce its ownership interest in the project so it can proceed.

For utilities, a small reactor has several advantages, starting with cost. Small reactors are expected to cost about $5,000 per kilowatt of capacity, or $750 million or so for one of Babcock & Wilcox's units. Large reactors cost $5 billion to $10 billion for reactors that would range from 1,100 to 1,700 megawatts of generating capacity.

While large reactors are built on site, a process that can take five years, the mPower reactors would be manufactured in Babcock & Wilcox's factories in Indiana, Ohio or Virginia and transported by rail or barge. That could cut construction times in half, experts believe.

Because they could be water-cooled or air-cooled, mPower reactors wouldn't have to be located near large sources of water, another problem for big reactors that require millions of gallons of water each day. That could open up parts of the arid West for nuclear development.

The first units likely would be built adjacent to existing nuclear plants, many of which were originally permitted to have two to four units but usually have only one or two.

Down the road, utilities could replace existing coal-fired power plants with small reactors in order to take advantage of sites already served by transmission lines and, in some cases, needed for grid support. Like any other power plants, these small reactors could be easily hooked up to the power grid.

One of the biggest attractions, however, is that utilities could start with a few reactors and add more as needed. By contrast, with big reactors, utilities have what is called "single-shaft risk," where billions of dollars are tied up in a single plant.

Another advantage: mPower reactors will store all of their waste on each site for the estimated sixty-year life of each reactor.

Nuclear development moves at a glacial pace. The next wave of large reactors won't begin coming on line until 2016 or 2017, at the earliest. The first certification request for a small reactor design is expected to be Babcock & Wilcox's request in 2012. The first units could come on line after 2018.

However, some experts believe that if the industry embraces small reactors, nuclear power in the U.S. could become pervasive because more utilities would be able to afford them.

"There's a higher likelihood that there are more sites that could support designs for small reactors than large ones," said David Matthews, head of new reactor licensing at the Nuclear Regulatory Commission.

That twist has some observers worried. "Nuclear power requires high-level security and expertise to operate safely," said Edwin Lyman, senior staff scientist for the Union of Concerned Scientists. "It seems like something that should be concentrated rather than distributed" or dispersed.

Experts believe small reactors should be as safe, or safer, than large ones. One reason is that they are simpler and have fewer moving parts that can fail. Small reactors also contain a smaller nuclear reaction and generate less heat. That means that it's easier to shut them down if there is a malfunction.

"With a large reactor, the response to a malfunction tends to be quick, whereas in smaller ones, they respond more slowly" which means they're somewhat easier to control, said Michael Mayfield, director of the advanced reactor program at the Nuclear Regulatory Commission. Once on site, each reactor would be housed in a two-story containment structure that would be buried beneath the ground for added security. They would run round the clock, stopping to refuel every five years instead of eighteen to twenty-four months, like existing reactors.

For communities looking for job creation, the smaller reactors promise fewer jobs than a large plant, which offers 700 to 1,000 permanent jobs. Small plants would have to satisfy the same security and safety standards as large plants but likely would require a somewhat smaller work force because they would run much longer between refueling outages.

Some critics are convinced that nuclear power will never be cost effective, no matter what the size. Amory Lovins, founder of the environmental think tank the Rocky Mountain Institute, said it's a "fantasy" to imagine that small reactors will be any better than big ones. He notes that nuclear energy is inherently expensive because of the special precautions that must be taken in the handling of nuclear fuel and nuclear waste, which are radioactive, not to mention the tight security at nuclear plants. Also, there still is no permanent federal site for nuclear waste.

The electricity industry was burned once before by nuclear power, and many utilities remain skittish.

Forty out of 48 utilities that issued debt for nuclear projects during the past construction cycle—twenty to thirty years ago—suffered credit hits in the aftermath of the Three Mile Island accident in 1979, most with downgrades of four notches, said Moody's Investors Service.

Now some of these same companies are looking at the nuclear option again. Energy Northwest is a wholesale utility in Richland, Wash. It's the successor to the Washington Public Power Supply System, which acquired the unfortunate nickname of "Whoops," after it canceled construction of two partly built reactors in the 1980s.

At the time, the utility thought demand would grow briskly. Instead, the economy slowed and so did demand. Nuclear plant costs for the five units it planned to build swelled to nearly $24 billion in 1982 from $5 billion in the 1970s. That set the stage for WPPSS's $2 billion bond default, at the time the largest in U.S. history.

Today, Energy Northwest is talking to NuScale Power Inc. in Corvallis, Ore., about a reactor design which measures 15 feet by 60 feet. Each unit would be capable of turning out 45 megawatts of electricity.

Jack Baker, Energy Northwest's head of business development, says he was initially skeptical about small reactors because of the "lack of economies of scale." But he says he now thinks small reactors "could have a cost advantage" because their simpler design means faster construction and "you don't need as much concrete, steel, pumps and valves."

"They have made a convert of me," he says.

Babcock & Wilcox's roots go back to 1867 and it has been making equipment for utilities since the advent of electrification, even furnishing boilers to Thomas Edison's Pearl Street generating stations that brought street lighting to New York City in 1882.

Based in Lynchburg, Va., the company has been building small reactors for ships since the 1950s. In addition to reactors for U.S. Navy submarines and aircraft carriers, it built a reactor for the USS *NS Savannah*, a commercial vessel which is now a floating museum in Baltimore harbor. It also built eight big reactors in the past construction cycle, including one for the ill-fated Three Mile Island plant.

When a U.S. nuclear revival looked imminent, the company debated what role it could play.

"Instead of asking, 'How big a reactor could we make?,' this time, we asked, 'What's the largest thing we could build at our existing plants and ship by rail?'" said Christofer Mowry, president of Modular Nuclear Energy LLC, Babcock's recently created small-reactor division. "That's what drove the design."

As interest in small reactors grows, other makers of big reactors are dusting off old designs.

Westinghouse, a unit of Toshiba Corp., is taking another look at its 335-megawatt reactor called Iris. Mario Carelli, Westinghouse chief scientist, said his firm is considering marketing Iris to nations with small grids, "where a big reactor won't fit." He figures that's 80% of the world's grids.

Many obstacles remain. The NRC still is reviewing certification requests for five big reactors and won't be able to consider certifications of small reactors until its work load lightens. But Mr. Matthews of the NRC says he expects the commission will review as many as four small-reactor designs in the next two or three years.

Meantime, interest in small reactors is likely to grow.

"If we can't figure out how to build large plants economically, then small ones may be the way to go," said Ronaldo Szilard, director of nuclear science and engineering at the Idaho National Lab, part of the Department of Energy.

Viewpoint 6

> *"The enormous technical and financial risks involved in the construction and operation of new nuclear power plants make them prohibitive for private investors."*

New Nuclear Power Plants Are Cost Prohibitive

Julio Godoy

In the following viewpoint, Julio Godoy cites studies in Europe and the United States and discusses the enormous costs involved in planning, building, and operating new nuclear plants. Godoy explains that new plants take longer to build than other power plants and are unlikely to turn a profit for the first twenty years. Potential construction delays and ballooning costs as evidenced by the Olkiluoto plant in Finland pose a major risk for investors, which, Godoy warns, if not offset by very high consumer costs and government subsidies, make new nuclear plants economically unfeasible. Godoy is a Guatemalan-born investigative journalist.

As you read, consider the following questions:

1. What are the five major risks for developers of nuclear power plants, according to the viewpoint?

Julio Godoy, "Nuclear Does Not Make Economic Sense Say Studies," *Inter Press Service*, February 12, 2010. http://ipsnews.net.

2. Why is the Olkiluoto 3 plant in Finland a warning, according to the author?
3. What is the necessary construction budget for a 1,600 megawatt nuclear power plant, according to French energy expert Thibaut Madelin?

The enormous technical and financial risks involved in the construction and operation of new nuclear power plants make them prohibitive for private investors, rebutting the thesis of a renaissance in nuclear energy, say several independent European studies.

New Nuclear Plants Are "Corporate Killers"

The risks include high construction costs, likely long delays in building, extended periods of depreciation of equipment inherent to the construction and operation of new power plants and the lack of guarantees for prices of electricity.

Adding to these is the global meltdown and the consequent cautious behaviour of investors and also fiscal and revenue difficulties of governments in the industrialised countries, say the studies.

In the most recent analysis on the feasibility of new nuclear power plants, the Citibank group concludes that some of "the risks faced by developers . . . are so large and variable that individually they could each bring even the largest utility company to its knees financially."

The Citibank paper, titled "New Nuclear—The Economics Say No," lists five major risks developers and operators of new nuclear power plants must confront. These risks are planning, construction, power price, operational, and decommissioning. According to the study, most governments in industrialised countries today have only "sought to limit the planning risk" for investors.

But, while it is "important for encouraging developers to bring forward projects, [planning] is the least important risk financially," the survey goes on. According to the Citibank group, the most important risks are construction, power price, and operational. The paper dubs these risks "the corporate killers."

Environmental activists would add safety issues as another major risk—both the handling of highly radioactive nuclear waste and the likelihood of accidents at nuclear power stations.

High Investment Cost Leads to High Consumer Prices

The Citibank bases its conclusions on estimated costs of construction and operation and in the necessity of setting too high electricity prices for consumers, and which have seldom been reached in the past.

According to the paper, the costs of constructing a new nuclear power plant range between 2,500 to 3,500 euros (3,420 US dollars) per kilowatt hour.

For an average 1,600 megawatt (MW) unit, such a range leads to construction costs of up to 5.6 billion euros (7.6 billion dollars). "We see very little prospect of these costs falling and every likelihood of them rising further," the study says.

To meet such costs, the operator would need a guarantee of constant electricity prices around 65 euros (88.9 dollars) per MW/hour for a long period of time.

The Citibank paper cites the British case where prices at that level on a sustained basis have occurred only 20 months during the last 115 months. "It was a sudden drop in power prices that drove British Energy to the brink of bankruptcy in 2003," the survey recalls.

Waiting for a Profit

Another survey of the so-called renaissance of nuclear power, carried out by physicist Christoph Pistner for the German Institute for Applied Ecology, comes to similar conclusions.

In the paper "Renaissance of nuclear energy," Pistner argues that developers "must finance in advance and for an unusual long period of time the huge construction costs of a new nuclear power plant."

In an interview with IPS [Inter Press Service], Pistner said that most power plants have to be running for at least 20 years to reach the operation period free of depreciation and impairments costs. Only after this period, a nuclear power plant starts yielding returns.

In addition, Pistner said, developers of nuclear power plants are confronted with yet another risk: "The industry disposes of little references on the buildings costs of new nuclear power plants because there are very few units in construction."

Construction Delays and Exploding Costs

Actually, there is a new nuclear power plant that serves as a warning example of the risks involved in such a project: the nuclear power plant of Olkiluoto 3 in Finland, under construction since 2004.

Although the plant was supposed to have started delivering electricity in May 2009, its completion was postponed several times in the past two years. On Feb. 11, the Olkiluoto 3 project manager Jouni Silvennoinen announced in Helsinki that the plant's start "may be pushed back further than June 2012, which is the current deadline confirmed by the equipment manufacturer."

The manufacturer is the French state-owned company AREVA. The plant was ordered by the Finnish company TVO.

Olkiluoto 3 is also facing an explosion of construction costs. Initially, it was estimated that the plant's construction would cost three billion euros (4.1 billion dollars)—but now the bills amount to well over 5.3 billion euros (7.2 billion dollars). How much the plant is actually going to cost remains unclear.

These costs must be added to the revenues losses TVO had budgeted as electricity sales, but which were never realised due to the non operation of the plant.

The delays in completion and the explosion of costs have led to litigation between the Finnish operator TVO and the manufacturer AREVA.

The Global Financial Crisis Magnifies Construction Cost Issues

In yet another critical appraisal of the feasibility of new nuclear power plants, French energy expert Thibaut Madelin says that the uncertainties linked to the construction costs of such plants have been magnified by the global financial crisis, which makes such huge investments unlikely.

Madelin said that construction delays of nuclear power plants constitute the central argument against them. "You can build a combined cycle gas turbine with a capacity of 800 MW in four years, for a construction cost of some 550 million euros (752.4 million dollars)," Madelin told IPS.

"But for a nuclear power plant of 1,600 MW, you need at least eight years, and a construction budget of up to six billion euros (8.2 billion dollars)," Madelin added. "That means that the investor of a new nuclear power plant would start seeing some money only eight years after she invested a huge amount of money."

According to Madelin, "if the construction of a nuclear power plant lasts more than ten years, the project becomes a financial catastrophe." Figures by the International Atomic Energy Agency (IAEA) say that construction delays jumped from sixty-four months (more than five years) to 146 months (more than twelve years) between 1976 and 2008.

There Are Insurmountable Obstacles to a Nuclear Resurgence

In a recent commentary published by the IAEA, Sharon Squassoni, researcher at the U.S. Carnegie Endowment for International Peace, also concluded that the financial crisis and the construction costs constitute almost insurmountable obstacles to the renaissance of nuclear power.

"The current economic crisis could make financing nuclear power plants particularly difficult," Squassoni wrote. "Financing costs account for between 25 and 80 percent of the total cost of construction because nuclear power plants take much longer to build than alternatives."

For example, wind plants require eighteen months to build, combined cycle gas turbines need thirty-six months, but nuclear power plants take at least sixty months, Squassoni noted.

Squassoni warned that the global tightening of risk management standards in the wake of the current economic crisis could imperil the nuclear industry, "in particular, because a reactor entails such a large investment (between five billion and ten billion dollars per plant) relative to the typical financial resources of electric utilities."

No Subsidies Means No Plants

The Citibank paper, referring to the Olkiluoto 3 plant, points out that cost overruns and time slippages of even a fraction seen by TVO and AREVA would be more than enough to destroy the equity value of a developer's investment "unless these costs can be passed through somehow", an euphemism for state subsidies.

"Given the scale of these costs, a construction programme that goes badly wrong could seriously damage the finances of even the largest utility companies," the Citibank survey says.

The Citibank survey concludes that without taxpayers money there is "little if any prospect that new nuclear stations will be built . . . by the private sector unless developers can lay off substantial elements of the three major risks. Financing guarantees, minimum power prices, and/or government-backed power off-take agreements may all be needed if stations are to be built."

Viewpoint 7

> *"The nuclear sector is experiencing an overall renaissance . . . , but there are important countries that are lagging well behind."*

New Reactors—More or Less?

Steve Kidd

In the following viewpoint, Steve Kidd discusses the two stages of the nuclear renaissance: the success of existing nuclear plants, and the commission of new reactors. The industry is booming in Asia, Kidd asserts, but outside of Asia investment has dried up. Kidd lists several reasons for this lack of investment: the recession causing a drop in electricity demand, a lack of financing, a disinterest in environmental concerns, and fears of ballooning reactor costs increased by more efficient energy sources such as shale gas. The author suggests that the success of existing reactors will eventually lead to a renaissance in the West. Kidd is director of strategy and research at the World Nuclear Association.

As you read, consider the following questions:

1. What are the two stages of the nuclear renaissance, according to the viewpoint?
2. How did the recession impact the electricity demand, according to Kidd?

Steve Kidd, "New Reactors—More or Less?," *Nuclear Engineering International Magazine*, January 21, 2011. www.neimagazine.com.

3. How does the federal loan guarantee program factor into investment in new nuclear programs, according to Kidd?

In North America and western Europe, shale gas discoveries and cost escalations are pushing back the start of the nuclear renaissance. In the meantime, Asian economies are leaping ahead.

It is reasonable to talk about the nuclear renaissance in two discrete stages. Firstly, the industry had to prove that it could run the existing stock of reactors a lot better than it was doing in the late 1980s and early 1990s. Indeed, if it hadn't done this, many of them would have closed down by now with the onset of electricity liberalisation in many countries. Much improved performance has now been accomplished almost universally, with reactors running at higher utilisation rates, more safely and also benefiting from power uprates and licence extensions. But the most important point is that operating reactors today are proving to be excellent cash cows in many countries, in fact to the extent that politicians are seeking additional ways to tax them (for example in Sweden, Belgium and now Germany). But if existing reactors resemble friendly ATMs, what is to stop stage two occurring, in other words that seemingly elusive time when additional reactors are commissioned in major nuclear countries, with some new countries gaining them for the first time?

It is undoubtedly true that this vital second level, a wave of new nuclear construction to parallel the experience of the late 1970s and early 1980s, has proved somewhat slow to get going. The IAEA reports that 65 new countries are now considering nuclear power; but it is unlikely that many will commission reactors unless there is a revival of construction in the more established markets. Most of the existing nuclear nations, however, are still merely talking about new reactors, rather than rushing forward to start construction. Nuclear critics may say that this talk is no more than a lot of hot air, and the mooted renaissance is dead. So what is delaying new reactors and could it be fatal?

If we make a comparison with two years ago, it is clear that prospects for new reactors in several countries now don't look as promising as they did then. This is, however, balanced by the incredible performance of China, which has within the past few years started work on more than 20 additional reactors and with ever more expansive plans announced for the future. So looking on a world scale, forecasters have not been cutting their anticipated numbers of new reactors to be online in 2020 or 2030—but there has been a notable switch in the market composition. The rise of China is clearly the big story, but the balance in the whole nuclear new build market has continued to swing sharply towards Asia. The expected rise of India and several possible new Asian nuclear countries are additions to the established programmes in Japan and Korea. So the nuclear sector is experiencing an overall renaissance if you talk of global orders for plant and equipment, but there are important countries that are lagging well behind.

The reasons for the slowdown in plans outside Asia can be discussed under three headings, namely the impact of the world economic recession, some specific changes in energy markets and finally some important developments in nuclear power itself.

One important impact of the recession has been a slowdown in electricity demand growth—indeed, world electricity demand fell in 2009 for the first time since 1945, despite rapid growth continuing in China and other developing countries. This decline was concentrated in the OECD countries and, in itself, has had a major impact on all energy investment plans, not just in nuclear. But in itself, this is likely to be only a delaying factor; demand is already returning to growth and the need to replace old, dirty generation assets remains. But the demonstration that power demand can fall as well as rise is a warning that prices can also be volatile, a message that is of concern to anyone planning projects like nuclear which require some certainty on future power prices—after all, there is only billions of kWh of power to sell, and nothing else.

Within the recession, the fact that financing has become more difficult must also have an impact on large projects like nuclear reactors that have huge upfront costs and long project cycles which carry a large variety of risks. Interest rates are now relatively low, but obtaining money has become more difficult, as lenders are drawing in their horns. The major impact of this in nuclear can be seen in Eastern Europe where a number of long-established projects are struggling to find finance, notably Belene in Bulgaria and the additional reactors at Cernavoda in Romania. Some potential backers have pulled out, perhaps because of electricity offtake uncertainties as much as finance cost and availability. Elsewhere in Western Europe, including the UK, likely investors are financially-strong utilities like EDF, E.On, Vattenfall, GDF Suez and RWE, who have the ability to invest in large projects. The position in the United States is clearly not so favourable as even the largest nuclear utilities are too small to undertake a project alone, so leaving consortia as the only route.

Another area where the recession has had a notable impact is on the importance (or not) of environmental considerations. It would be a parody to say that harder economic times have forced people to forget about the environment, but climate change and global warming sometimes now sound like old news and firm commitments to doing anything about them have possibly wavered. The difficulties of getting any traction in the US Senate and Congress on emissions trading is a case in point—at a time when the economy is sick, effectively imposing a financial burden on important heavy energy-consuming areas with strong lobby groups becomes difficult. This may, again, be only a temporary phase which evaporates when the economy improves, but getting governments to help achieve their emissions targets via strong policy actions is proving as difficult as pessimists always anticipated. The subsidies to renewable energy remain, but even wind power companies are beginning to feel the pinch with some factory closures and deep scepticism about the economics of offshore projects.

Turning to energy markets, the key development here has been within natural gas. The economics of generating power through combined cycle gas turbines (CCGTs) is almost 100% to do with the gas price. Investing in these has also been something of a no-brainer for power companies over the past 10 or so years. In liberalised power markets, they tend to be the marginal supplier (getting turned on and off to cope with peaks and troughs in the load) and the power prices at the time have to cover their marginal costs of operation (mainly gas). So provided the (relatively low) capital investment costs of the plants can be covered in the good times, investing in CCGTs is a relatively safe option. This is, however, threatened by high gas prices; new projects look unattractive if one assumes high prices will remain. In addition, plants have run at low operating levels when power demand has been low.

Gas prices have historically been closely related to oil prices, and obviously there is an important complication on how the gas gets to the customer, either piped or liquified. Gas prices escalated sharply with oil prices in 2006–8, and initially fell back with oil thereafter. But they have continued falling, while oil has stabilised at about $80 per barrel. The reason for this is largely down to the discovery of large quantities of unconventional shale gas, particularly in the United States and technological advances which demonstrate that these can be exploited cheaply and brought to market. The potential magnitude of these unconventional resources outside the United States is not known with any great precision but the geological settings which favour them are extensive. The outlook for gas prices has therefore changed significantly, with many commentators now expecting them to be in the $4–6 per million BTU range going ahead, rather than $8–10 as expected before.

This poses a major problem for nuclear projects, at least where cheap gas is available and its future supply relatively secure. Capital investment costs for 1000We of power generation capacity are about one fifth for a CCGT plant compared with nuclear. The simple option in this case is to build gas—indeed, the quickest way to save carbon emissions in the US electricity sector could be to shut down all the old and dirty coal plants and replace them with new CCGTs. Such a decision may have long term implications for sustainable use of valuable resources (the gas will clearly become exhausted at some stage). But particularly in liberalised markets where a quick return on investment is prized, more gas plants will probably be built.

The major development within the nuclear sector itself that is influencing future reactor plans is the continued adverse news on escalating reactor costs and the delay to the construction schedules for the EPRs in Finland and France. This is where the experience in Europe and North America compared with Asia is so different. Although making cost comparisons is hazardous, the latest IEA and OECD-NEA report on projecting electricity generating costs show a major gap, with reactors in China and Korea built for around $2000 per kW on an overnight (i.e. excluding interest costs during construction) basis, while Europe and North America examples are assessed at two to three times this level. China and Korea are also mainly reliant on relatively expensive liquified natural gas, so the economic equation is very much slanted towards more nuclear build.

It is clear that something has to be done in the western world about the high capital costs of nuclear—at the levels being quoted today, the project risks are such that only the biggest utilities (as mentioned above) can consider investing. The answer has to do with more standardization in designs and the regulatory system, but the experience of series construction of advanced reactor designs in China should push some costs down. But new nuclear reactors are huge civil engineering projects, involving a lot of local labour and locally produced materials such as concrete, so it is impossible to cut some areas of the cost structure. Simplified reactors built in volume in both Europe and North America are surely the answer—both of conventional evolutionary large designs but also note the renewed interest today in small and medium sized reactors (SMRs).

Within the United States, the delays to the federal loan guarantee programme are often cited as an important additional factor slowing new nuclear projects. It is generally agreed that with the gas price and reactor cost issues, loan guarantees are essential, although they in themselves cannot be sufficient to determine whether a nuclear project flies or not. After all, the $5 billion or so it costs to build a new reactor still have to be paid back—the guarantee simply makes the financing easier (and so cheaper).

We are therefore currently living in two nuclear worlds, with rapidly-developing Asian countries experiencing nuclear booms similar to those in the West in the late 1970s and early 1980s, whereas the rest of the world is still feeling the water again. Ultimately there should be a link between the two, when the experience of construction in Asia translates elsewhere. China and India will likely join Japan and Korea as significant exporters of nuclear technology and components, but their project management experiences are also crucial. For the reactor owners and operators in the West, the key thing is to carry on running their reactors very well and eventually the penny will drop—putting into operation new large nuclear generating units with low, stable and predictable operating costs is maybe not so difficult after all.

> *"Congress should not create a host of new federal subsidies and other incentives that will shield the [nuclear] industry from the considerable costs of investing in this highly risky technology."*

Government Subsidies Mask the Real Costs and Risks of Nuclear Power

Union of Concerned Scientists

In the following viewpoint, the Union of Concerned Scientists argues against new government subsidies that bolster the nuclear industry, as this would mask the actual costs of nuclear power, making it seem more profitable while actually deferring the cost to taxpayers. The viewpoint discusses existing subsidy programs such as the loan guarantee, a depreciating fund, investment and production tax credits, and risk insurance programs. The group maintains that the United States needs an agency that oversees and limits such subsidy programs and prioritizes support for technologies that counteract global warming efficiently. The Union of Concerned Scientists is a non-profit organization that advocates for a healthy and safe environment.

Union of Concerned Scientists, "Nuclear Power Subsidies Will Shift Financial Risks to Taxpayers," June 2010. www.ucsusa.org.

As you read, consider the following questions:

1. According to the viewpoint, how should the Clean Energy Bank prioritize funding?
2. What is the new proposed accelerated depreciation period, according to the viewpoint?
3. What does the viewpoint indicate is covered by the current insurance policy under the Energy Policy Act of 2005?

The nuclear power industry is seeking tens of billions in new subsidies and other incentives in federal climate and energy legislation that would shift massive construction, financing, operating and regulatory costs and risks from the industry and its financial backers to U.S. taxpayers. Congress should reject these overly generous subsidies to this mature industry whose history of skyrocketing costs and construction overruns already has resulted in two costly bailouts by taxpayers and captive ratepayers—once in the 1970s and 1980s when utilities cancelled or abandoned more than 100 plants, and again in the 1990s when plant owners offloaded their "stranded costs." Massive new subsidies will only further mask nuclear power's considerable costs and risks while disadvantaging more cost-effective and less risky carbon reduction measures that can be implemented much more quickly, such as energy efficiency and many renewable energy technologies.

The nuclear industry already will benefit from considerable subsidies provided by the Energy Policy Act of 2005 and from a price on carbon emissions. These subsidies should be more than adequate to allow the industry to demonstrate whether it can build a limited number of "first mover" units, on time, on budget, and operate them safely (as recommended by numerous experts), and which the initial loan guarantees and other subsidies included in the 2005 Act were designed to support. However, proposals in pending legislation go way beyond what is needed to accomplish that goal. To illustrate this point, this analysis quantifies key nuclear subsidies in two Senate bills: The American Power Act (APA) and the American Clean Energy Leadership Act (ACELA).

There Should Be No New Subsidies for the Nuclear Industry

Using conservative capital cost estimates ($7,085/kW including financing) and assuming eight new reactors are built over the next fifteen years, we estimate that the nuclear industry could obtain new subsidies worth in excess of $40 billion, or $5 billion per reactor, if a broad range of industry handouts are included in pending climate and energy legislation. If all thirty-one reactors for which the Nuclear Regulatory Commission (NRC) has received or expects to receive applications are built, total proposed subsidies to the industry could be worth between $65 billion and $147 billion. While not all subsidies will be available to every project, the collective impact of these handouts will be large because companies will be able to pick and choose among a wide range of subsidies best suited to a variety of partnership and financial structures. Given the industry's poor financial track record and history of cost overruns, cancellations and bailouts, Congress should not create a host of new federal subsidies and other incentives that will shield the industry from the considerable costs and risks of investing in this highly risky technology by shifting those costs and risks to taxpayers.

The Clean Energy Bank Must Have Clear and Effective Limits

If Congress creates a new federal financing entity called the Clean Energy Deployment Administration (CEDA) to promote the domestic development and deployment of clean energy technologies, then it must include adequate taxpayer protections that would limit the overall size of the fund as well as the amount of credit support that could go to any one technology. Congress should not exempt CEDA from the Federal Credit

Reform Act (FCRA), which would allow the fund to provide potentially unlimited loan guarantees to large, well-capitalized entities that are able to pay their estimated subsidy costs up front. Congress should also require CEDA to prioritize financial support for technologies that will reduce the most global warming emissions per dollar invested. These provisions modifications are necessary to reduce the overall risk of default to taxpayers and mitigate negative impacts on the competitiveness of more economic and environmentally acceptable alternatives. Finally, new loan guarantees should be limited to helping emerging technologies cross the "valley of death" to be deployed on a large scale and become commercially viable. With 104 operating reactors in the United States and new reactor designs that are largely unchanged from those in commercial operation, reactors based on designs currently pending before the NRC should not be classified as emerging technologies. *As proposed, CEDA could provide virtually unlimited loan guarantees; the potential value could be worth more than $3 billion per reactor and between $24 billion to $94 billion to the industry.*

The Loan Guarantee Program for New Reactors Should Not Expanded

Proposals to triple the authority for nuclear loan guarantees through the existing Loan Guarantee Program from $18.5 billion to $54 billion should be rejected. The proposed new loan guarantees would result in allocating more than half of the fund to nuclear energy and shift the risks of financing the construction of risky, capital-intensive nuclear power plants from private industry to taxpayers. This would substantially lower the cost of capital for new plant construction and could significantly advantage high cost nuclear power plants over cleaner and more cost-effective alternatives such as energy efficiency and renewable energy. *The proposed expansion in DOE [Department of Energy] loan guarantees could be worth more* *than $3 billion per reactor and between $24 billion to $26 billion to the industry.*

The Accelerated Depreciation Period for New Reactors Should Not Be Reduced

Reducing the period from 15 years to five years would allow the nuclear industry to claim substantially larger tax deductions and much lower tax payments for assets with a life expectancy exceeding 40 years. This would significantly reduce the industry's tax burden and increase its after-tax profit. The nuclear industry claims that such a provision would put nuclear power on par with renewable energy technologies under the federal tax code; however, the dollar value of the subsidy would be much greater for nuclear than for renewables because of the large disparity between the actual asset life and the depreciate life of these projects. *This subsidy could be worth as much as $700 million per reactor and between $6 billion to $23 billion to the industry.*

New Reactors Should Not Receive a Ten Percent Investment Tax Credit (ITC)

This provision would significantly reduce the industry's tax liability while tilting emerging energy markets towards large, capital intensive projects and away from less risky, more cost-effective clean energy alternatives. An ITC is more appropriate than a production tax credit (PTC) for smaller projects to lower transaction costs and as a temporary measure when financing is hard to obtain. This provision would allow companies to claim "progress expenditures" in advance of the plant actually being completed, regardless of how long it takes to build them or whether they ever generate power. Similarly, Congress should not provide federal payments for new reactors in lieu of tax credits to municipal and cooperative utilities. This would require taxpayers to make payments to cover 10 percent of the investment of publicly owned and cooperative utilities that decide to build new reactors, constituting a massive handout to these entities due to the large disparity in size and cost vs. other existing and emerging low-carbon technologies. *Together, these subsidies could be worth as much as $800 million per reactor and between $6 billion to $24 billion to the industry.*

The Production Tax Credit for New Reactors Should Not Be Expanded

The Energy Policy Act of 2005 already provides a 1.8 cent per kilowatt tax credit for the first 6,000 MW of nuclear power to come on line. Proposals to increase the limit to 8,000 MW or to allow tax exempt entities to allocate their available credits to private partners would greatly expand the value of this subsidy to the industry. *An expanded subsidy could be worth as much as $1.4 billion per reactor and $10 billion to the industry.*

Tax Exempt Bonds Should Not Be Used for Public-Private Partnerships for New Reactors

This provision would enable publicly owned utilities to issue tax free, low-cost bonds for nuclear plants developed jointly with private interests. Depending upon ownership structure, plants could be eligible for a broad combination of subsidies. Because it is not possible to project what percentage of plants would be financed using this mechanism, we did not estimate a total value to the industry. *However, the estimated value of the proposed Build America Bonds Act and other tax-exempt bond financing for the Vogtle reactor project in Georgia is $4.1 billion.*

Federal Regulatory Risk Insurance for Nuclear Plants Should Not Be Expanded

The Energy Policy Act of 2005 already provides $2 billion in total coverage for up to six reactors to shield them against costs associated with regulatory and legal delays, a protection that is not

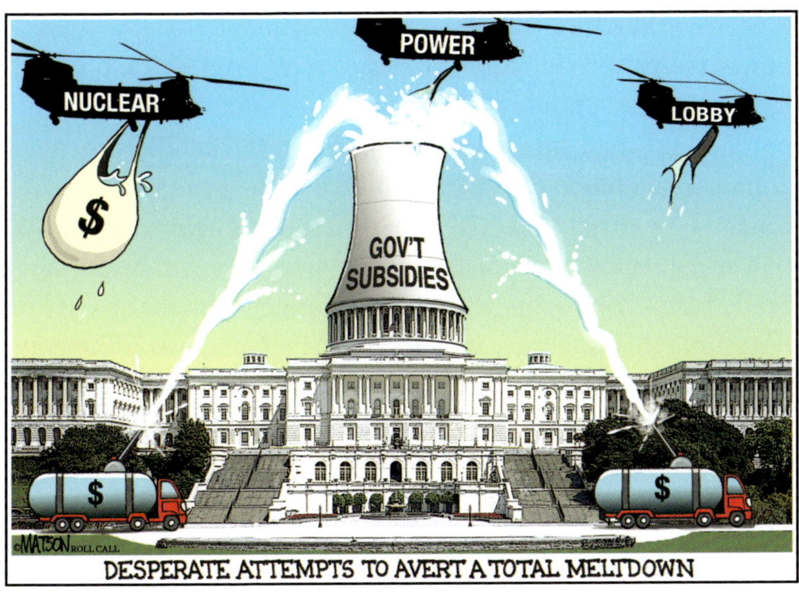

Desperate Attempts to Avert a Total Meltdown Cartoon. © R.J. Matson cartoons, reprinted with permission.

available to other low carbon technologies. Congress should not expand the coverage to $6 billion and twleve reactors or expand the circumstances and time frame under which this coverage will be provided. Providing for direct payments from the federal government to reactor developers for delays in NRC construction and licensing proceedings would shield reactor developers from the costs associated with certain regulatory and legal proceedings that could lead to delays in new reactor construction, certification and operation by shifting these costs to taxpayers. *This subsidy is worth as much as $500 million per reactor and $4 billion to $6 billion to the industry.*

New Nuclear Reactors Already Benefit from Generous Taxpayer Subsidies

An earlier case study by Earth Track of the proposed new reactor at Calvert Cliffs in Maryland, which will be co-owned by Constellation Energy and Électricité de France, provides a window into the subsidies already available to new nuclear power plants through loan guarantees and production tax credits provided by the Energy Policy Act of 2005, as well as other more established subsidies including federal liability insurance already available to the nuclear industry. The analysis shows the range of financial incentives that directly benefit new nuclear power plants and demonstrates that taxpayers will be the largest de facto investor in new nuclear projects under current law. Based on this analysis, the financial benefits currently available to Calvert Cliffs are estimated at between $631 million and more than $1 billion per year.

Periodical and Internet Sources Bibliography

The following articles have been chosen to supplement the diverse views presented in this chapter.

Patricia Brett — "The Dilemma of Aging Nuclear Plants," *New York Times*, October 19, 2009.

Zoey Casey — "Is Nuclear Power an Economic Failure?," *Green Chips Stocks*, March 14, 2012.

Mark Clayton — "Nuclear Power's New Debate: Cost," *Christian Science Monitor*, August 13, 2009.

Paul Davidson — "Nuclear Power Inches Back into Energy Spotlight," *USA Today*, March 30, 2009.

Charles D. Ferguson — "Do Not Phase Out Nuclear Power—Yet," *Nature Reviews*, March 23, 2011.

Eric Fontinelle — "The Economic Reasons Behind Nuclear Power," *Investopedia*, April 8, 2011.

James A. Lake, Ralph G. Bennett, and John F. Kotek — "Next Generation Nuclear Power," *Scientific American*, January 26, 2009.

Jason Morgan — "Comparing Energy Costs of Nuclear, Gas, Wind and Solar," *Nuclear Fissionary*, April 2, 2010.

John Vidal — "Nuclear Power is an Expensive Gamble That May (or May Not) Pay Off," *Guardian*, February 17, 2012.

Matthew L. Wald — "As Reactors Age, the Money to Close Them Lags," *New York Times*, March 20, 2012.

Bryan Walsh — "Is Nuclear Power Viable?," *Time*, June 6, 2008.

For Further Discussion

Chapter 1

1. Rod Adams uses the Fukushima Daiichi disaster to show that the risks involved with nuclear power plants are manageable. Jim Riccio uses the same incident to argue the exact opposite. What are the facts they use to support their respective arguments? How do they interpret these facts?
2. Leslie Corrice, Darshak Sanghavi, and Brian Moench discuss the safety risks of exposure to radiation, arguing three distinct viewpoints: exposure to low levels of radiation is safe, exposure to radiation is never safe, and it is impossible to say. After reading these three viewpoints, who do you agree with and why? Does your answer affect your opinion on the medicinal uses of radiation? Why or why not?
3. Nuclear non-proliferation involves the attempt to ensure that rogue nations or terrorists do not build or purchase nuclear arms. Given that the technology involved in nuclear power plants could potentially be used for non-peaceful purposes, do you think nuclear plants pose a national safety risk? Read the viewpoints of the World Nuclear Association and Najmedin Meshkati to inform your response.

Chapter 2

1. Is nuclear energy vital to ensure the ever-growing energy supply of the future? Do you think future energy needs can be met without nuclear power? Consider the viewpoints of George Monbiot and Mark Clayton to guide your response.
2. Can nuclear power help fight global warming? Use the viewpoints of Colin McInnes—who argues that it can—and the Natural Resources Defense Council—which argues that it cannot—to help formulate your opinion.

Chapter 3

1. Mycle Schneider, Antony Froggatt, and Julie Hazemann assert that the nuclear industry has been declining for decades and will never be economically sustainable. Jack Spencer warns that abandoning nuclear power has wide-ranging ramifications, not only for energy production, but for countries such as the United States that have built industries around supplying materials, parts, and resources for nuclear power. After reading these viewpoints, what do you think? What effects might abandoning nuclear power have on the economy? Should nuclear power continue to be supported? Why or why not?
2. Ferdinand Banks asserts that nuclear power is affordable and represents a far greater cost savings than increasing energy efficiency or reducing energy consumption. Joseph Romm argues that nuclear power is so costly that it could never serve as a viable major source of energy, and the industry is incapable of surviving financially without large government subsidies. Which author do you think provides the best-supported and most compelling argument? Why? Could there be an approach to the economic issues surrounding nuclear power that combines their views? If so, what might that look like? If not, why not?

Organizations to Contact

The editors have compiled the following list of organizations concerned with the issues debated in this book. The descriptions are derived from materials provided by the organizations. All have publications or information available for interested readers. The list was compiled on the date of publication of the present volume; names, addresses, phone and fax numbers, and e-mail and Internet addresses may change. Be aware that many organizations take several weeks or longer to respond to inquiries, so allow as much time as possible.

American Nuclear Society (ANS)

555 North Kensington Ave.
La Grange Park, IL 60526
(800) 323-3044 • fax: (708) 352-0499
website: www.new.ans.org

The American Nuclear Society (ANS) is a non-profit, international, scientific, and educational organization that works to promote the awareness and understanding of the application of nuclear science and technology. Since its founding in 1954, ANS has developed a membership composed of approximately eleven thousand engineers, scientists, administrators, and educators representing 1,600 plus corporations, educational institutions, and government agencies. The ANS website contains a public information window that provides publications such as news briefs and position statements.

Beyond Nuclear

6930 Carroll Ave., Suite 400
Takoma Park, MD 20912
(301) 270- 2209 • fax: (301) 270-4000
e-mail: info@beyondnuclear.org
website: www.beyondnuclear.org

Beyond Nuclear is an advocacy organization that seeks to educate and activate the public about the connections between nuclear power and nuclear weapons and the need to abandon both to safeguard our future. The Beyond Nuclear team works with diverse partners and allies to provide the public, government officials, and the media with information about the dangers of nuclear power. The group's website offers overview information about each aspect of nuclear power as well as other publications such as fact sheets, reports, press releases, congressional testimony, articles, and videos. Recent publications include two fact sheets: *The Nuclear Power Nuclear Weapons Link* and *New Nuclear Power Plants: An NRDC Fact Sheet.*

Greenpeace International
Ottho Heldringstraat 5 1066 AZ
Amsterdam, The Netherlands
fax: 31 (0) 20 718 2002
e-mail: supporter.services.int@greenpeace.org
website: www.greenpeace.org

Greenpeace is an independent global campaigning organization that acts to change attitudes and behavior in order to protect and conserve the environment and promote peace. The group's goals include promoting an energy revolution to address climate change and working for the elimination of nuclear weapons. Greenpeace is opposed to nuclear power, and its website provides numerous reports and publications relevant to this issue. Recent publications include *The Economics of Nuclear Power* and *The Nuclear Calendar—365 Reasons to Oppose Nuclear Power.*

International Atomic Energy Association (IAEA)
Vienna International Centre
PO Box 100
1400 Vienna, Austria
(431) 2600-0 • fax: (431) 2600-7

e-mail: Official.Mail@iaea.org
website: www.iaea.org

The International Atomic Energy Association (IAEA) is the world's center of cooperation in the nuclear field. It was set up in 1957 as the world's "Atoms for Peace" organization within the United Nations family. The IAEA works with its member states and multiple partners worldwide to promote safe, secure, and peaceful nuclear technologies. The organization publishes books, booklets, newsletters, fact sheets, and magazines such as the *IAEA Bulletin*.

National Resources Defense Council (NRDC)

40 West 20th Street
New York, NY 10011
(212) 727-2700 • fax: (212) 727-1773
website: www.nrdc.org

The National Resources Defense Council is a grassroots environmental action group that aims to safeguard the earth and the people, plants, and animals inhabiting it. The group focuses on issues such as combating global warming, developing clean energy sources, reviving the world's oceans and defending endangered wildlife to foster a sustainable world. The group's work involves education, legislation, and activism.

Nuclear Energy Institute (NEI)

1776 I Street NW, Suite 400
Washington, DC 20006-3708
(202) 739-8000 • fax: (202) 785-4019
website: www.nei.org

The Nuclear Energy Institute (NEI) is the policy organization of the nuclear energy and technologies industry that participates in the national and global policy-making process. NEI's objective is to ensure the formation of policies that promote the beneficial uses of nuclear energy and technologies in the United States and around the world. The group's website contains a section that addresses the key issues in the nuclear power debate as well as a resources section that directs researchers to various reports, brochures, graphics, and other publications. The group also publishes a monthly newsletter, *Nuclear Energy Insight*.

Union of Concerned Scientists

Two Brattle Square
Cambridge, MA 02238-9105
(617) 547-5552 • fax: (617) 864-9405
website: www.ucsusa.org

The Union of Concerned Scientists was founded in 1969 by a group of scientists and students at the Massachusetts Institute of Technology to protest the militarization of scientific research and promote science in the public interest. Since its founding UCS has focused on nuclear weapons and nuclear power, but it is also concerned with issues such as global warming, clean energy, food and agriculture, and invasive species. The UCS website provides information about nuclear power and its risks and problems. Recent UCS publications include *Nuclear Power: A Resurgence We Can't Afford* and *Nuclear Power Loan Guarantees: Another Taxpayer Bailout Ahead?*

US Nuclear Regulatory Commission

Washington, DC 20555-0001
(800) 368-5642
website: www.nrc.gov

The US Nuclear Regulatory Commission (NRC) was created as an independent agency by Congress in 1974 to help the United States to safely use radioactive materials for beneficial civilian purposes. The NRC regulates commercial nuclear power plants and other uses of nuclear materials, such as in nuclear medicine, through licensing and inspection. The NRC's website provides information about the location and regulation of US nuclear reactors as well as issues such as radioactive waste disposal and nuclear security.

US Department of Energy—Office of Nuclear Energy

1000 Independence Ave., SW
Washington, DC 20585
(202) 586-4403
e-mail: Contact.NE@nuclear.energy.gov
website: www.ne.doe.gov

The Office of Nuclear Energy within the US Department of Energy promotes nuclear power as a resource capable of meeting the United State's energy, environmental, and national security needs by resolving technical and regulatory barriers through research, development, and demonstration. The website contains a public information center, which provides publications, press releases, reports, congressional testimony, and other information. Publications include fact sheets titled *Nuclear Energy—An Overview* and *Generation IV Nuclear Energy Systems*.

World Nuclear Association (WNA)

22a St. James's Square
London SW1Y 4JH
United Kingdom
44 (0)20 7451 1520 • fax: 44 (0)20 7839 1501
e-mail: wna@world-nuclear.org
website: www.world-nuclear.org

The World Nuclear Association (WNA) supports the global nuclear energy industry and promotes the use of nuclear power worldwide. The WNA website includes information about next generation nuclear designs and also offers various publications, including position statements, speeches, and reports such as *Ensuring Security of Supply in the International Nuclear Fuel Cycle* and *The New Economics of Nuclear Power*.

Bibliography of Books

John P. Banks and Charles K. Ebinger, eds.	*Business and Nonproliferation: Industry's Role in Safeguarding a Nuclear Renaissance*. Washington, DC: Brookings Institution Press, 2011.
David Bodansky	*Nuclear Energy: Principles, Practices, and Prospects*. New York: Springer, 2008.
Helen Caldicott	*Nuclear Power Is Not the Answer*. New York: New Press, 2007.
Martin Cohen	*The Doomsday Machine: The High Price of Nuclear Energy, the World's Most Dangerous Fuel*. New York: Palgrave Macmillan, 2012.
Stephanie Cooke	*In Mortal Hands: A Cautionary History of the Nuclear Age*. London: Bloomsbury, 2009.
Gwyneth Cravens and Richard Rhodes	*Power to Save the World: The Truth About Nuclear Energy*. London: Vintage, 2008.
Pete V. Domenici	*A Brighter Tomorrow: Fulfilling the Promise of Nuclear Energy*. Lanham, MD: Rowman & Littlefield, 2007.
Charles D. Ferguson	*Nuclear Energy: What Everyone Needs to Know*. New York: Oxford University Press, 2011.

Trevor Findlay	*Nuclear Energy and Global Governance: Ensuring Safety, Security and Non-Proliferation.* London: Routledge, 2012.
Juan José Gomez Cadenas	*The Nuclear Environmentalist: Is There a Green Road to Nuclear Energy?* New York: Springer, 2012.
Gabrielle Hecht	*Being Nuclear: Africans and the Global Uranium Trade.* Cambridge, MA: MIT Press, 2012.
Alan M. Herbst and George W. Hopley	*Nuclear Energy Now: Why the Time Has Come for the World's Most Misunderstood Energy Source.* Hoboken, NJ: Wiley, 2007.
Maxwell Irvine	*Nuclear Power: A Very Short Introduction.* New York: Oxford University Press, 2011.
Eric Jeffs	*Greener Energy Systems: Energy Production Technologies with Minimal Environmental Impact.* Boca Raton, FL: CRC Press, 2012.
Maggie Koerth-Baker	*Before the Lights Go Out: Conquering the Energy Crisis Before It Conquers Us.* Hoboken, NJ: Wiley, 2012.
Jay H. Lehr	*Nuclear Energy Encyclopedia: Science, Technology, and Applications.* Hoboken, NJ: Wiley, 2011.

James A. Mahaffey	*Atomic Awakening: A New Look at the History and Future of Nuclear Power*. Trenton, TX: Pegasus, 2009.
Arjun Makhijani	*Carbon-Free And Nuclear-Free: A Roadmap for U.S. Energy Policy*. Muskegon, MI: RDR Books, 2007.
Will Mara	*The Chernobyl Disaster: Legacy and Impact on the Future of Nuclear Energy*. Salt Lake City, UT: Benchmark Books, 2010.
Richard Martin	*SuperFuel: Thorium, the Green Energy Source for the Future*. New York: Palgrave Macmillan, 2012.
Ewan McLeish	*The Pros and Cons of Nuclear Power*. New York: Rosen Central, 2007.
Laura Nader, ed.	*The Energy Reader*. Hoboken, NJ: Wiley-Blackwell, 2010.
Reese Palley	*The Answer: Why Only Inherently Safe, Mini Nuclear Power Plants Can Save Our World*. New York: Quantuck Lane Press, 2011.
Christine Shrader-Frechette	*What Will Work: Fighting Climate Change with Renewable Energy, Not Nuclear Power (Environmental Science and Ethics Policy)*. New York: Oxford University Press, 2011.

Neil Singer	*Wonders of Nuclear Fusion: Creating an Ultimate Energy Source*. Albuquerque: University of New Mexico Press, 2011.
Brice Smith	*Insurmountable Risks: The Dangers of Using Nuclear Power to Combat Global Climate Change*. Muskegon, MI: RDR Books, 2006.
Benjamin K. Sovacool and Scott Victor Valentine	*Contesting the Future of Nuclear Power: A Critical Global Assessment of Atomic Energy*. Singapore: World Scientific Publishing Company, 2011.
Benjamin K. Sovacool and Scott Victor Valentine	*The National Politics of Nuclear Power: Economics, Security and Governance*. London: Routledge, 2012.
Frank R. Spellman and Melissa L. Stoudt	*Nuclear Infrastructure Protection and Homeland Security*. Lanham, MD: Government Institutes, 2011.
Galen J. Suppes and Truman Storvick	*Sustainable Nuclear Power*. Burlington, MA: Academic Press, 2006.
Mariko Takahashi and Toshihiko Kastuda	*Fukushima Nuclear Power Plant Disaster: What Happened in March 2011*. Tokyo: The Asahi Shimbun, 2011.

William Tucker	*Terrestrial Energy: How Nuclear Energy Will Lead the Green Revolution and End America's Energy Odyssey*. Savage, MD: Bartleby Press, 2008.
Robert Vandenbosch and Susanne E. Vandenbosch	*Nuclear Waste Stalemate: Political and Scientific Controversies*. Salt Lake City: University of Utah Press, 2007.
Spencer R. Weart	*The Rise of Nuclear Fear*. Cambridge, MA: Harvard University Press, 2012

Index

G

H

I

J

K

S